Hare Krishna in the Modern World

Published in 2013 by Arktos Media Ltd.

Published in the United Kingdom.

This book is printed on acid-free paper.

ISBN 978-1-907166-47-1

BIC classification:
Hinduism (HRG)
Educational: Religious studies: Hinduism (YQRN3)

Editors: Graham Dwyer & Richard J. Cole
Co-Editor: John B. Morgan
Cover Design: Andreas Nilsson
Layout: Daniel Friberg

Cover photo: His Holiness Radhanath Swami being interviewed by the BBC
at Bhaktivedanta Manor's Janmashtami festival, 10 August 2012.
Copyright 2012 Bhaktivedanta Manor Archives.

ARKTOS MEDIA LTD
www.arktos.com

Hare Krishna
in the Modern World

Reflections by Distinguished Academics
and Scholarly Devotees

Compiled, Edited and Introduced
by
Graham Dwyer and Richard J. Cole (Radha Mohan Das)

ARKTOS
London
2013

Table of Contents

Introduction

The Hare Krishna movement, also known as the International Society for Krishna Consciousness (ISKCON), is now in its fifth decade of life. Since its founder, A.C. Bhaktivedanta Swami Prabhupada, first came to the West in 1965, and since establishing his Society in 1966, the movement has undergone major change in terms of its organisational structure and leadership, in terms of its economic base, and in terms of its missionary activities. Over a period of nearly 50 years it has gone through the turbulent loss of its charismatic founder, and has experienced schisms, financial crises, and a notable decline in key areas of preaching and proselytising.

Yet the Krishna Consciousness movement has survived these difficulties and continues to evolve in the postcharismatic phase of its development. Whether or not the movement will continue to hold on to its existing members, as well as attract new converts, and what the movement must do in order to endure or flourish, are critical questions with which many academics, particularly in the fields of Religious Studies, History of Religions and Sociology of Religion, are concerned today. The same questions are also of major import confronting leaders within the movement itself and with which they must now grapple. These questions about the central issues and challenges faced by ISKCON and found also at the heart of much contemporary scholarly debate are what this book explores.

This book is a compilation of in-depth reflections on the Hare Krishna movement, reflections elicited during interviews with distinguished academics and with highly respected researchers and writers in the movement. It also includes a separate essay, which offers a historical and comparative perspective on ISKCON's development as a new religious organisation, and in its final remarks the book provides comment on the legacy of Prabhupada's movement. The arguments and viewpoints of the interviewed experts shed new light on the status of ISKCON in today's varied landscape of spiritual practices and aspirations, as do the their first-hand accounts of how the Hare Krishna movement has changed and developed in order to respond to the challenges it has encountered and continues to confront in the modern world. In terms of what is at stake here and in terms of the future prospects of ISKCON, the views of all these contributors furnish this book both with valuable insights and with fresh understandings.

The seven experts interviewed here who express their views have been selected not only because of their specialists' knowledge, but also because of their direct experience of the Hare Krishna movement from its early nascent period through to what it has become today. Interviews with them, recorded on cassettes over a period of eighteen months (from November 2009 to April 2011) and later transcribed and edited for this volume, have all been arranged in the book using a common set of categories or subheadings, as each recorded interview followed the same structure, involving a uniform schedule of semi-structured questions. This helps the reader to easily move through the interview material, enabling the reader to also compare and to contrast the various perspectives, arguments and thoughts articulated by the expert contributors. The categories or subheadings employed throughout the book's interview material are: (1) First Encounter; (2) Changes, Developments and Future Prospects; (3) Indian and Non-Indian Devotees; (4) Theological Challenges: Conservative and Liberal Perspectives; (5) Women and Gender Roles; and, finally, (6) Concluding Thoughts and Reflections.

In the section on "First Encounter," the book's seven interviewed experts offer reflections on their initial contact with the Hare Krishna movement and the early days of ISKCON in the West. "Changes, Developments and Future Prospects" has a major focus on organisational or structural dimensions of ISKCON, with attention given to how the Society has both evolved and how it continues to undergo transformation in a variety of different socio-political contexts internationally, as well as what such changes mean for ISKCON as it endeavours to go forward. "Indian and Non-Indian Devotees" deals largely with economic features and with cultural practices from the perspective of the growing and dynamic relationship between Indian Hindus and non-Indian converts, the relationship itself involving challenges but also being key to the very life and stability of the Hare Krishna movement. In "Theological Challenges: Conservative and Liberal Perspectives," the focus is primarily on the fundamentalist and revisionist trends found within ISKCON today, but it also looks at major schisms that have occurred in the Krishna Consciousness movement, and explores the extent to which competing factions or groups may be thought still to pose a threat to it. The penultimate section on "Women and Gender Roles" both reviews the place of women in ISKCON and examines their relationship with men, not only in terms of their different but sometimes overlapping roles, but also in terms of issues of power, ritual duties, or service and spiritual aspirations.

Finally, "Concluding Thoughts and Reflections" offers points of discussion on issues not directly covered in the book's main themes and topics, but which the interviewed contributors wished to have included.

Comments given by the interviewed specialists on the various topics presented in the book, however, vary in terms of the amount of time devoted to the treatment of any one specific issue or theme, reflecting the approach adopted during the interview process itself. Indeed, as its design aimed to ensure flexibility and freedom for the expert participants to develop particular lines of argument as well as to express their personal viewpoints, this has been of great benefit, adding much to the richness and diversity of the ideas discussed. But while the scope of the book has a broad base, in matters pertaining to ISKCON in the modern world it is equally comprehensive.

Inevitably, perhaps, a book of this kind will include some differences of opinion, but they are not highly pronounced in the interview material; indeed, what is particularly striking throughout is the overall level of consensus that is found. Much agreement is seen on a wide range of issues, with the expert interviewees drawing attention to many similar factors. These include, for example, thoughts about how ISKCON has increasingly embraced the disciplines and practices of academic study and academic conventions of critique. But this is also viewed as an area of ongoing challenge, as it necessitates intellectual reflection that invariably requires a degree of self-criticism. Moreover, while it is made clear in the book that ISKCON is becoming a broader and much more inclusive organisation, one that engages in serious theological debate, as well as offering spiritual and intellectual training to its members, the issue of how ISKCON can accommodate opposing theological interests remains an important challenge. Furthermore, as ISKCON is becoming more and more firmly embedded in mainstream society and continues to deepen its relationship with Hindus in diaspora, as well as widen its relationship with other religious groups in various interfaith forums and events, these developments are seen by the book's contributors as signalling ISKCON's growing maturity. Yet they are equally held to be problematic; for, as ISKCON moves along this trajectory while attempting to retain an identity framed by an essentially anti-modernist philosophical outlook, there will inevitably be complexities of boundary construction, and this is considered to be an ongoing challenge for ISKCON too. In addition, for ISKCON to ensure the transmission of its teachings and practices to its youth and to a new generation of followers whose ideas are also shaped and informed by the values of wider society, particularly values of equality—values that celebrate gender rights and rights of sexual orientation or sexual expression, for example—ISKCON will increasingly have to find new ways of achieving flexibility. And such flexibility or the ability to resist isolationist tendencies that marked ISKCON's beginnings is viewed by the book's contributors as being of major import if ISKCON is to continue to retain its appeal.

In all these matters, then, the arguments and thoughts articulated in the book offer forceful and persuasive conclusions about ISKCON's future prospects in the modern world. All the expert contributors agree that ISKCON remains essentially successful as a religious organisation, one that is likely to grow and to flourish in the future, though undoubtedly involving struggle. Since there has been much new and renewed interest in the Krishna Consciousness movement in recent years, this book will thus be of importance to students and scholars, not only students and scholars of the Hare Krishna movement in particular but also those who have an interest in new religious movements in general. It is hoped that the clear, frank and informed reflections articulated in this book will be welcomed and received as a useful resource. For those who wish to understand the Hare Krishna movement in the modern world, and for those who are especially concerned to understand the complex challenges with which the movement will continue to grapple with now and in the future, the book will be especially valuable.

As a final remark, it should be pointed out that, as the interviews for this book had almost neared their completion, A.C. Bhaktivedanta Swami Prabhupada's younger Bengali contemporary, Bhaktivedanta Narayana Maharaja, passed away. Since debate about Narayana Maharaja as a potential threat or source of opposition to ISKCON has been an important focus in this book, his demise in December 2010 is a significant development, and makes comment about him, particularly in relation to ISKCON's future prospects, especially significant now. How ISKCON as a new religious movement will continue to be shaped in its postcharismatic phase will be affected by the departure of Narayana Maharaja as well as by a variety of other key figures and factors explored in this work. As such this book offers much food for thought from which, it is hoped, academic readers concerned with ISKCON or new religious movements, as well as scholars in the fields of Religious Studies, Sociology of Religion and the History of Religions will greatly benefit.

1. Sociological Reflections on the History and Development of the Hare Krishna Movement

By Professor E. Burke Rochford, jr.

Introduction

Like the other contributors to this volume I have spent a large portion of my life involved with ISKCON and its members. My research began in 1975 when, as a naïve graduate student, I found my way to studying the ISKCON community in Los Angeles. This proved a difficult undertaking because during this period, one was either a devotee, or a *karmie* or "demon," to use the colourful language of the day to characterise outsiders. Negotiating entrée into the community represented a personal challenge as well as a professional one that raised numerous questions about my self-understanding and identity (see Rochford 1985: 21-45). Today a social scientist would find it far easier to gain access to ISKCON's communities, a fact that speaks to the changes that have occurred over the past 37 years.

ISKCON, and the now broader Hare Krishna movement, have undergone profound change since Prabhupada established ISKCON in New York City in 1966 (see Dwyer and Cole 2007). During this era the United States was facing an unpopular war and many of America's youths were protesting the war as well as the materialism that defined American society. As the sociologist Robert Bellah argued, the 1960s and early 1970s exposed the "horrors of modern history" resulting in "mass defection from the common understandings of American culture and society" (1976: 333). In the midst of societal unrest some young people in and outside of the United States came to accept ISKCON's anti-modern philosophy and lifestyle. However, as Dr. King reminds us, Prabhupada's mission involved more than "world rejection" (Wallis 1984: 9-20), as he also sought to "re-spiritualise the world and engage in a campaign of cultural conquest." Thus ISKCON sought to transform the secular society by modelling a way of life that placed Krishna in the centre. It was these attributes of social protest and world transformation that defined ISKCON as a new religious movement, and which led the media and the anti-cult movement to portray ISKCON as a controversial and threatening "cult."

Until the early and mid-1980s ISKCON devotees in North America, Western Europe, and in other parts of the world lived communally and engaged in a variety of spiritual practices meant to ensure their spiritual realisation. Individually chanting the names of Krishna (*japa*), and participating in activities such as congregational chanting (*kirtan*), deity worship (*puja*), preaching and book distribution (*sankirtan*), as well as public chanting (*harinam*), defined the everyday lives of ISKCON's members. Involvement in the outside society was considered *maya* (illusion) and a threat to the fragile "devotional creepers" of the young men and women who were drawn to Prabhupada and his Krishna Consciousness movement.

Today ISKCON is a very different religious organisation. Its former *outward* opposition to mainstream society has largely faded into the background and most devotees no longer actively seek to bring about a worldwide spiritual renewal. Instead, gaining social acceptance and increased legitimacy have replaced ISKCON's previous radical goals. Accommodation to the outside world defined by ongoing alignment with mainstream institutions and cultural conventions have prevailed over the past two decades or so. Interfaith alliances, charitable work, environmental activism, the growing significance of ISKCON's Indian Hindu congregation, the demise of the movement's *gurukula* system in favour of public education, growing gender equality, and the diminished authority of ISKCON's leadership, all point to fundamental changes in ISKCON's religious and organisational cultures. As a consequence of these and related changes, the scope and influence of the movement's beliefs and mission have progressively narrowed with personal religiosity, devotee relationships and family responsibilities being dominant concerns for most devotees (see Rochford 2007a).

Several contributors to this book suggest that many of the changes that ISKCON has undergone point to its growing maturity as an established religious organisation. While ISKCON conservatives would likely find reason to debate such a conclusion, it is nonetheless true that many of these changes were strategic and practical responses to ISKCON's decline beginning in the early 1980s. Necessity born of organisational weakness has pushed ISKCON's leaders and members toward greater societal accommodation in order to bolster the organisation's viability. However, the fact that ISKCON has survived for nearly 50 years, despite significant change, is a testament to the devotees' resilience and to the power of Prabhupada's teachings and vision for ISKCON.[1]

---

1   Success has been defined in varying ways by scholars of utopian communities and religious movements. Rosabeth Moss Kanter (1968: 502), for example, defines

In the remainder of this essay I reflect as a sociologist on three key issues raised by the editors and contributors to this volume: (1) Changes in ISKCON's Structure and Purpose; (2) Succession, Leadership and the Problem of Authority; and, (3) the Ongoing Hinduisation of ISKCON. My attempt is to offer both a historical and comparative perspective on ISKCON's development as a new religious movement. Before turning to these specific issues, however, I first provide a framework for understanding change in new religious movements.[2]

New Religions and Transformation

Out of frustration and disappointment devotees sometimes express the view that ISKCON must be unique; that surely other religious groups have not faced the turmoil and dramatic changes that ISKCON has undergone, especially since Prabhupada's passing in 1977. However, the fact is that all of the major new religions of the sixties era (e.g., the Unification Church, Children of God/The Family) have experienced organisational decline and increased accommodation to mainstream societies (see e.g., Amsterdam 2004; Barker 1995; Chancellor 2000; Introvigne 2000: 47; Mickler 2006).[3]

success in terms of survival. If a utopian community exists for a generation, or at least 25 years, it is considered successful. Rodney Stark (1987, 1996) defines success in terms of power and influence. New religious movements are successful to the extent that they "dominate one or more societies" (1987: 12). Obviously such a definition rules out the vast majority of new religions that have arisen historically, a fact that lessens the empirical usefulness of Stark's definition. Moreover, unlimited growth and societal influence may come at the expense of original teachings and organisation (Wilson 1987: 30-31). Viewed from within, such changes may well be interpreted as evidence of failure.

2 Joshua Greene and Dr. Edith Best raise important questions about sociological studies of ISKCON. More specifically, both find reason to challenge some of my sociological writings on the movement. Greene argues that my book *Hare Krishna Transformed* is not "adequately objective" and that it unfairly skews readers' impressions of ISKCON by painting an overly narrow view of the movement and its devotees. Dr. Best raises other issues suggesting that I tend to over-generalise my findings. She correctly asserts that ISKCON has developed differently worldwide and thus my discussion of ISKCON in North America should not be taken as definitive. These criticisms remind me that insider and outsider perspectives, as well as disciplinary and theoretical frameworks, ultimately represent different ways of both "seeing" and "not seeing." As a sociologist trained in the study of social movements, I am especially alive to issues and events that have influenced ISKCON's development as a new religious movement. While I see no reason to apologise for this, I realise that my perspective on ISKCON (like all perspectives) is inevitably "incomplete" and "skewed." For self-critical and reflective discussions of my ISKCON research, see Rochford 1992, 2001a.

3 ISKCON is unique in one respect, as the movement has experienced an ongoing crisis of authority since Prabhupada's death in 1977, a point I discuss later.

From exclusive, communal, and high commitment organisations, each became congregationally-based with members who hold widely varying degrees of commitment and levels of involvement.[4] Thus, over time high-tension religious groups tend to become domesticated and transform into low-tension religions. Just such a pattern is predicted by the longstanding sect-to-church model. By progressively aligning with dominant cultural patterns and social institutions, new religions cast off their outsider status and become "respectable," as the sociologist of religion Roy Wallis (1984: 89) explains, "It is widely recognised that such a pattern of initial zealous rejection of the world and later progressive accommodation to it is characteristic of many religious movements which later settle into thoroughly respectable denominations."

Not all unconventional religious groups, of course, follow a path toward denominationalism and instead maintain their distinctive religious culture (see e.g., Kraybill 2001 on the Amish).[5] In other cases, religious groups undergoing secularisation face insurgency and schism as those committed to a strict and high-tension religion break away and form a new organisation that is often hostile toward the parent group and its leadership (Finke and Stark 1992; Lewis and Lewis 2009). Therefore, the struggle between the forces of resistance and accommodation help shape the developmental course of both sectarian groups and new religious movements (e.g., see Mauss 1994 and Ammerman 1995 on resistance and change in the Mormon Church and Southern Baptist Convention, respectively).

Because new religious movements challenge as well as offer an alternative to mainstream values and institutions, creating and sustaining

---

4   In 2001, The Children of God/The Family's membership included 8,900 "Charter members" residing communally as full-time members, 3,100 "Fellow members" living and working outside of the movement, and more than 64,000 "Outside members," ranging from "live-out disciples" to those whose involvement is limited to financial contributions (Shepherd and Shepherd 2002: 5-6). After The Family completed restructuring in 2003 its Charter member population declined by 2,360. Less committed Charter members became Fellow members or newly created Missionary members. Among the trends related to decline in member commitment was a decrease in communal households, outside employment, children attending secular schools, and expectations that second-generation members would not maintain the Charter members' standards of discipleship (Amsterdam 2004).

5   The Amish have both resisted and accommodated to American society, a pattern that Kraybill (2001) describes as the "riddle" of Amish culture. Accommodation is provided for, but only if it does not undermine important elements of the Amish religious culture, including social and familial relationships. Much of the negotiation that occurs—whether involving accommodation or resistance—centres on maintaining the traditional family farm, given its economic and cultural significance to the Amish way of life.

oppositional religious cultures are vital to realising their world-trans-forming objectives (Iannaccone 1988; Lofland 1987; Rochford 2007b: 172-74, Stark 1996). As Stark (1996: 137) argues, "In order to grow, a religious movement must offer a religious culture that sets it apart from the general, secular culture." In engaging the project of cultural development, new religions seek to create structures, practices, and symbols that promote group solidarity while, at the same time, segregating members from the perceived threats posed by the secular society. Yet evidence suggests that new religions have often struggled in their efforts to develop robust religious cultures and the institutional structures that support them. This failure stems largely from an inability to construct internal domestic cultures supportive of family life. This became a particularly acute problem when many of the new religions of the 1960s came to have substantial numbers of children, in some cases outnumbering their parents' generation (Barker 2004:98).

Lacking internal structures of support, parents and children have had little choice but to seek employment, schooling, and recreation within the conventional society (Amsterdam 2004; Chancellor 2000; Introvigne 2000: 46-47; Rochford 2007a). Not surprisingly perceptions of the outside society changed accordingly as images of a "corrupt" and "demonic" system become difficult to sustain when substantial numbers of first-and second-generation members alike find their everyday lives bound by mainstream involvement. In making peace with the world, however, religious movements subvert their radical goals and increase the likelihood for internal factionalism, defection, organisational switching and schism (Finke and Stark 1992). Moreover, accommodation also alters a group's recruitment niche as those seeking a strict and high tension religion go elsewhere to be replaced by people wanting a less strict and more conventional religious experience (Stark and Finke 2000: 205).

Changes in ISKCON's Structure and Purpose

Beginning in the early 1980s, ISKCON's communal structure began to disintegrate in North America and shortly thereafter in other ISKCON locations as well when revenues from book distribution declined spectacularly, leaving the movement's temple communities in financial jeopardy (Rochford 1985, 2000).[6] Devotee parents and their children were

---

6 Book distribution in North America expanded yearly until 1976 and provided significant sums of money in support of ISKCON's temple communities. One conservative estimate suggests that ISKCON's North American communities grossed more than $13 million between 1974 and 1978 on hardback books alone (Rochford

forced out of the communal fold to establish self-supporting households. Adults found employment in the outside labour market and large numbers of children transitioned into state-supported schools after ISKCON's *ashram*-based *gurukula* system collapsed due to a lack of funds in the mid-1980s (Rochford 2007a: 66). Thereafter, the nuclear family displaced communalism as ISKCON's defining structure of social organisation and ISKCON became a congregationally-based religious organisation (Rochford 2007a: 62-66).

The shift in the organisational structure of the movement led to a number of specific changes of note. The demise of communalism meant that the household largely replaced the temple as the central location for devotees' religious practice. Apart from the Sunday programme, which attracts many Indian congregational members, ISKCON's temples, as Dr. Valpey suggests, remain largely empty during the week. In place of attending the temple, most devotees worship deities at home instead. Religious life, therefore, became increasingly privatised as work and family responsibilities made it difficult, if not impossible, for householders to maintain their previous levels of collective religious practice (i.e., attending the early morning temple programme). These obligations also meant that most devotees had little choice but to reduce the amount of volunteer work they performed on behalf of their local temple community (Rochford 1995, 2001b, 2007a: 70-71). Young people transitioning into non-ISKCON schools from the *ashram-gurukula* also tended to turn away from their ISKCON involvement as they sought acceptance from their non-devotee classmates (Rochford 2007a: 97-114).

As Kripamoya Dasa points out, in recent years devotees have created new structures to facilitate their collective worship and to promote devotee association.[7] Devotees in the United Kingdom have formed informal house groups where they gather for *kirtan* (congregational singing), philosophical discussion, and taking *prasadam* (sanctified vegetarian food), often without any involvement or endorsement by ISKCON authorities. In the London area alone there are approximately 30 house groups operating with 10 to 60 participants in each group. Similar gatherings can also be found in North America, and presumably elsewhere, especially among

---

1985: 174-76). By 1980, however, book distribution had fallen to one-quarter of its peak and the corresponding loss of revenues proved devastating to ISKCON's communities. The demise of book distribution occurred later in other parts of the ISKCON world but the financial implications and resulting consequences mirrored those that occurred in North America (Rochford 2000, 2011a).

7   For Kripamoya Dasa's work on devotee house groups in the UK and for other writings by this senior ISKCON leader, see www.deshika.wordpress.com.

devotees who for various reasons remain estranged from ISKCON, or who live at a considerable distance from an ISKCON temple community (see e.g., Rochford 1989 for a discussion of the Kirtan Hall).

The emergence of the nuclear family also provided devotee women with new opportunities to redefine their roles and to achieve greater equality with devotee men. In most religious traditions places of worship are governed by male clergy or other male elites, even as women carry out much of the practical work of maintaining the congregation as a religious community. Family households by contrast have traditionally been the domain of women, a fact that affords them greater leverage in negotiating gender and family roles (see e.g., Gallagher 2003 for a discussion of the ways that scripturally mandated "male headship" is negotiated and reconstructed within Evangelical families). For this and other reasons,[8] ISKCON's traditionally-defined gender ideology has been reworked, and increasing numbers of female *and* male devotees now accept many of the gender norms associated with modern Western societies (see Rochford 2007a: 133-34).[9]

The declining significance of the temple community has produced a number of institutional dilemmas for ISKCON with regard to missionary outreach and religious training. No longer are devotees committed to going out on *sankirtan* like they were in the past. Two-thirds of the respondents to the North American Prabhupada Centennial Survey agreed that "I have little desire to go out in public and distribute books and preach" (Rochford 2007a: 209). Although commitment to public outreach

8 Changes in attitudes about women's roles and place in ISKCON also shifted in the direction of gender equality when ISKCON's communities began facing (literally) manpower shortages in the 1980s and 1990s, and women were called on to serve as temple presidents and in other positions of authority in the absence of men. As this occurred, traditionalist ideas about women became increasingly difficult to sustain, and most were set aside or reinterpreted to legitimate women's new responsibilities in ISKCON's management structure (see Rochford 2007a: 132-35).

9 Findings from the 1996 North American Prabhupada Centennial Survey suggest how both men and women devotees have come to accept greater gender equality. Three-quarters of all women and two-thirds of all men agreed that qualified women should have the opportunity to serve as temple presidents and GBC representatives. More than two-thirds of both women and men also agreed that women should be allowed to chant in the temple with men, have equal access to the deities during worship, and have the same opportunities as men to realise their potential in devotional service (work in ISKCON). In addition, a similar majority of both men and women agreed that: performance, not gender, should be the criterion for placement in an ISKCON position; women are the spiritual equals of men; Prabhupada never intended women devotees to be treated as other than equal to devotee men; and, that men's attitudes have become more accepting of devotee women over time (see Rochford 2007a: 133-34). For more details on the methodology and findings from the Prabhupada Centennial Survey, see Rochford (1999).

has declined, many devotees do discuss Krishna Consciousness with non-devotees at work or school, or in other parts of their everyday lives. Yet the fact remains that few non-Indians are choosing to join ISKCON and most temples no longer maintain formal programmes to educate and train newcomers. This contrasts sharply with the past when *bhaktas* and *bhaktins* received formal and informal training in the *ashram* in the presence of seasoned devotees who served as their spiritual guides.

Today, religious education within ISKCON has taken on a different form. Following the trend of many established religious groups, seminars, workshops, and courses in Vaishnava philosophy and other topics have increasingly filled the void. *Bhakti Sastri* courses of several weeks' length are held in a number of locations such as Bhaktivedanta College in Belgium, at ISKCON's Mayapur and Vrindavan India communities, and at New Vrindaban in West Virginia. Short-term workshops and seminars are also offered at major ISKCON festivals throughout the year. Every spring, for example, the New Vrindaban community hosts a three-day "Festival of Inspiration," which attracts as many as 700-800 devotees from around North America. A variety of workshops and classes are held that address Prabhupada's books as well as topics such as "Taking Krishna Consciousness out of the Temple," "Srila Jiva Goswami and Vedanta Philosophy," and "The Transcendental Mechanics of Chanting" (Rochford 2007a: 208-212).

The expansion of adult education has certainly been valuable but as Kripamoya Dasa observes, more needs to be done since most people do not join ISKCON—or any religious organisation for that matter—on the basis of theology alone. Joining is ultimately about making human connections. For as Lofland and Stark (1965) argue, religious conversion is a process whereby a person comes to believe what one's friends' believe (also see Snow and Phillips 1980). Establishing personal relationships, therefore, become critical to both developing and maintaining individual commitment in the context of *nama hatta* (house) groups as well as within ISKCON temple communities. Unfortunately, ISKCON's economic situation has too often meant that temple authorities are more concerned with attracting patrons than with nurturing a new generation of devotees committed to Prabhupada and his teachings.

Succession, Leadership and the Problem of Authority

Charismatic authority has been central to the emergence and development of new religious movements. Charismatic leaders face the ongoing task of sustaining their legitimacy in collaboration with followers.

Charisma thus grows out of social interaction between leaders and those who attribute charisma to them (Dawson 2002). More broadly, leader authority maintains legitimacy to the extent that rank and file members perceive themselves as active participants in the system of authority to which they are subject (Stark 1996: 139-40). Charismatic authority produces a relationship of emotional intensity which at the group level readily translates into high levels of organisational commitment, religiosity, and task performance as followers seek to realise the goals of the leader and his or her organisation (Dawson 2002: 82). But as Max Weber (1978: 246) makes clear, charismatic authority is inherently unstable and remains in its "pure" form only in the short run. Given this volatility, charisma must be institutionalised or risk implosion (Dawson 2002: 85).[10]

The effort to successfully carry forward the mission of a charismatic leader inevitably leads to pressures for more stable and bureaucratic forms of organisation, if only to counter the spontaneous *ad hoc* quality of charismatic authority (Wallis 1984: 108-10). Growth places limits on the ability of charismatic leaders to maintain their previous level of contact with followers, and the need for coordinated action requires specialists who can develop strategies, supervise followers, and delegate tasks essential to the success of the group. Moreover, as members become more invested in the group they tend to seek institutional structures that afford greater predictability and stability. This is especially true as members grow older, have families, and require greater security in their lives.

A major development in the life of any religious movement emerges upon the death of a revered charismatic leader. Some religious groups fade away with the passing of a charismatic founder (Kanter 1972: 118; Miller 1991), although most survive with only moderate disruption, especially when prior preparation affords a smooth transfer of power (Melton 1991:9-10). Among the more established new religions, Scientology, the Children of God/The Family, Transcendental Meditation, the Rajneesh Foundation International/Osho, Siddha Yoga Dham, as well as ISKCON have experienced the death of their charismatic founders. Yet only ISKCON experienced ongoing conflict over issues of authority in the

---

10 A clear example of this volatility can be seen in the case of former ISKCON guru Kirtanananda Swami and New Vrindaban. Kirtanananda's charisma was never routinised which contributed greatly to the violence, religious innovation, and ultimate transformation of the community in the mid-and-late 1980s (Rochford and Bailey 2006; Rochford 2011b; Rochford and Doktorski forthcoming). See also Dawson (2002: 92-94) for a discussion of the counteractive strategies employed by charismatic leaders to confront or deflect attempts to institutionalise their authority.

aftermath of Prabhupada's death in 1977.[11] One significant factor that separates ISKCON from the other groups is that guru authority is generally hostile to effective organisation because disciples are committed first and foremost to their gurus and only secondarily to an established organisation (Rochford 1985: 221-55, 1998). Therefore, succession for ISKCON involved immediate fragmentation as each of Prabhupada's 11 guru successors claimed independent authority, a situation that produced years of conflict.

Prabhupada's death in the fall of 1977 represented a major turning point for ISKCON's worldwide development. Unable to travel in the months prior to his passing, Prabhupada appointed 11 of his closest disciples to serve as *ritvik*-gurus. Following Prabhupada's demise, however, the appointed *ritvik*-gurus assumed the position of regular gurus, offering *diksha* (first) initiation to persons who accepted them as their spiritual master (Rochford 1998, 2009). Institutionally, the newly appointed gurus were accorded the same reverence and authority as ISKCON's founder. Having proclaimed themselves *acharya*s (heads of a religious institution), Prabhupada's successors considered themselves largely immune from the decisions and will of ISKCON's worldwide governance structure, the Governing Body Commission (GBC). As one insider concluded, "Indeed, the gurus with their status as sacred persons, a status constantly emphasised by formal deference and ceremonial honors, and their growing numbers of personally devoted followers, quickly eclipsed the GBC" (Ravindra Svarupa Das 1994: 27). To all intents and purposes, each of the 11 gurus led separate movements within their geographical zones, where they exercised exclusive political, economic, and spiritual authority (Rochford 1998: 104). Controversial from the beginning, the "zonal *acharya* system" existed for nearly a decade.

The GBC was only able to regain its political standing when a majority of the 11 gurus became embroiled in scandal and controversy during the late 1970s and 1980s (Rochford 1985: 221-55, 1998).[12] As might

---

11 By contrast, the death of the Children of God's founder David Berg in 1994 produced little in the way of internal conflict, as leadership was successfully transferred to Berg's wife Maria and to Peter Amsterdam (see Chancellor 2000). Amsterdam has played a central role in the administration of The Family while Maria has promoted the use of prophecy in planning and decision-making throughout the organisation (Shepherd and Shepherd 2006).

12 The GBC suspended three gurus in 1980 for improper behaviour. In 1982 ISKCON experienced its first major schism when the guru Jayatirtha left ISKCON with as many as 100 of his disciples. In 1984, after years of controversy surrounding him, Hamsadutta was expelled from ISKCON over allegations of drug use and weapons violations in California. In 1985 and 1986 three other gurus — Ramesvara, Bhagavan, and Bhavananda — were forced to resign their guruships after sexual

be expected, these guru scandals provoked serious questioning among ISKCON devotees about the guru institution and the appointment of Prabhupada's successors. They also resulted in large numbers of devotees defecting from the organisation and produced widespread calls for reform. Many who left ISKCON took up lives in the conventional society where they practiced Krishna Consciousness independently of ISKCON. Others chose to join forces with other Gaudiya Vaishnava organisations associated with Prabhupada's godbrothers in India. Most notable were B. R. Sridhara Maharaja and Narayana Maharaja, the latter being a disciple of Prabhupada's godbrother B. P. Keshava Maharaja (Rochford 2007a: 169-71, 2009: 269-73).

Under the leadership of senior Prabhupada disciples, many of whom were North American temple presidents, a reform movement successfully pressured the GBC in 1986 to make a number of changes in ISKCON's guru institution. Among the most important was expanding the number of ISKCON gurus, which effectively undermined the zonal *acharya* system because gurus could no longer lay claim to exclusive geographical zones. The GBC also ruled that the term *acharya* could only be used to refer to ISKCON's founder, Prabhupada. And, finally, the GBC restricted guru worship in ISKCON temples to Prabhupada exclusively. Thereafter, the number of gurus increased from 30 to 60 in 1990, and to 80 in 1993 (Squarcini and Fizzotti 2004: 26). Despite these reforms, however, controversy over the guru institution remained.

Beyond leader-initiated reforms, ISKCON also faced an influential grassroots movement determined to redefine the guru system. Supporters of the *ritvik* movement argued that people accepting initiation from a current ISKCON guru, in fact, were disciples of Prabhupada because Prabhupada had never appointed any of his disciples to serve as initiating (*diksha*) gurus but only as *ritvik*-gurus. In this role ISKCON's successor gurus were authorised to serve only as ceremonial priests initiating on Prabhupada's behalf. Such an interpretation meant that Prabhupada would remain as ISKCON's spiritual master even in death (Desai 1996).

Many devotees inside and outside ISKCON found themselves sympathetic toward the *ritvik* position in the face of ongoing scandal and controversy surrounding Prabhupada's successors. One in four (25%) full-time ISKCON members and half of the movement's congregational

---

misconduct and other charges were brought against them (Rochford 1985, 1998). In 1987 ISKCON authorities excommunicated Kirtanananda Swami, who led ISKCON's New Vrindaban community in West Virginia after murder and other charges were brought against him and other members of the community (Rochford and Bailey 2006; Rochford 2011b).

members (49%) and ex-members (56%) responding to the North American Prabhupada Centennial Survey (N= 281) agreed with the statement, "To my understanding, Prabhupada wanted the 11 *ritviks* he appointed to continue as *ritviks* after his departure" (Rochford 2007a: 173, 245n9).[13]

In the midst of growing support for the *ritvik* position, an organised countermovement developed to challenge ISKCON's guru system. The ISKCON Revival Movement (IRM) emerged in the late 1990s, claiming that ISKCON's gurus were neither authorised by Prabhupada nor qualified to serve in their positions. Thus, the IRM represents an insurgent group whose primary mission is to displace ISKCON's existing structure of religious authority in favour of restoring Prabhupada's position as ISKCON's only initiating guru. (For more details on the IRM, see Desai, Awatramani and Das 2004; Rochford 1998, 2007a: 171-75, 2009: 273-81).

Setting aside important theological questions about whether initiation requires a "living guru," the *ritvik* philosophy functionally restores authority to the guru institution (if not the current gurus), with Prabhupada serving as ISKCON's single source of religious authority. *Ritvik* gurus may fall from grace but the guru institution, so central to ISKCON's religious system, maintains its spiritually pure character in the form of ISKCON's founder, Prabhupada.

Although ISKCON authorities have aggressively confronted the "*ritvik* heresy" (Rochford 2009: 279-81), the movement's system of authority has nonetheless changed under the weight of guru scandals and the *ritvik* challenge.[14] The GBC passed a number of resolutions meant to redefine the authority of ISKCON's gurus in relation to Prabhupada. GBC resolutions have referred to Prabhupada as the "foundational *siksa* [instructing] guru for all ISKCON devotees" (1994), "preeminent *siksa* guru for every

---

13 Support for the *ritvik* position was somewhat less for devotees in Western and Northern Europe, with 20% of the full-time ISKCON members and 52% of ex-members agreeing with the statement (N=147). In Latin America, 45% of the full-time members agreed that Prabhupada wanted the *ritvik* gurus he appointed to remain as such after his death (N=70). Because survey questions dealing with the guru institution were only asked of initiated devotees, the number of congregational members who responded to the *ritvik* statement from Western/Northern Europe and Latin America was small, and I chose to exclude them from the analysis as a result. I did the same for ex-members from Latin America. Finally, questions addressing the guru institution were not asked on the questionnaire distributed in Eastern Europe at the request of ISKCON authorities.

14 In 2011 only two of Prabhupada's original 11 successors remained as initiating gurus. Moreover, after the number of ISKCON gurus increased to more than 80 following the reforms of 1986, still other gurus fell from their positions. Of the 104 ISKCON gurus appointed between 1977 and 2004, 34 were removed from their positions and an additional 14 were sanctioned by the GBC for misbehaviour (Rochford 2009: 268).

member of the institution" (1999), and the "preeminent and compulsory *siksa* guru for all Vaisnavas [gurus and disciples] in the [ISKCON] Society" (1999).

The Ongoing Hinduisation of ISKCON

By the mid-1980s ISKCON's communities in North America and in Western Europe were facing a sharp decline in membership and in financial resources. Few new recruits were joining and many of ISKCON's longstanding members had either defected or were practicing Krishna Consciousness more or less independently of ISKCON. Similar decline also occurred in Eastern Europe, beginning in the late 1990s, following a decade of sustained growth. In 2000 there were only about 750-900 residents living in 45 ISKCON centres in the United States (Squarcini and Fizzotti 2004: 70). The decline in book distribution revenues in the absence of alternative sources of economic support left many of ISKCON's communities struggling to survive. In the midst of decline, ISKCON's leadership sought ways to revitalise the movement and its temple communities.

To help overcome the lack of temple-based devotees, ISKCON communities in North America and Western Europe imported devotee labour from a number of developing countries to meet their needs (Rochford and Bailey 2006; Rochford 2007a: 180). While this helped offset labour shortages, persistent and serious financial problems remained. To ease the financial crisis, the leadership decided to develop more fully the movement's Indian Hindu congregation in locations having substantial immigrant populations.[15] Success at this effort is suggested by the fact more than 50% of ISKCON's approximately 50,000 member congregation in the United States is of Indian descent. In some major North American cities such as Atlanta, Chicago, Dallas, Los Angeles, New York, and Toronto the percentage of Indians in the congregation ranges upward to 80%. The

---

15 Indian immigration in the United States increased dramatically after President Lyndon Johnson rescinded the Oriental Exclusion Act in 1965. Between 1951 and 1960 less than 2000 Indians came to the US, a number that grew considerably after 1965 with 164,134 immigrating between 1971 and 1980 and 250,786 between 1981 and 1990. In 2000 there were 1.6 million Indian immigrants in the US, many located in major American cities and surrounding suburbs (Yearbook of Immigration Statistics 2004). A similar trend also occurred in Canada during the 1960s and 1970s when substantial numbers of South Asian professionals immigrated, only to be followed by Hindus from East Africa, South Africa, Fiji, Mauritius, Guyana, and Trinidad (Coward 2000: 152-53). Substantial immigration to Britain began years earlier after India gained its independence in 1947, and in 2009 there were 1.4 million people of Indian descent living in England, 480,000 of which were residing in London (Office of National Statistics, June 2009).

same applies to ISKCON's Bhaktivedanta Manor close to London where tens of thousands of Indian Hindus worship and attend major religious festivals.[16]

The involvement of large numbers of Indian Hindus within ISKCON represents a major change from the movement's early days when Indian people were typically ignored by the devotees when they came to the temple in part because Prabhupada did not want ISKCON to be overly identified with Hinduism. In a 1969 conversation with several of his followers at New Vrindaban, Prabhupada stressed that ISKCON was *not* a Hindu movement:

> I don't want a Hindu temple. Our constitution is different. We want everyone. Krsna consciousness is for everyone. It is not a Hindu propaganda. People may not understand. And actually, till now in our [ISKCON] society there is not a single other Hindu than me (laughter). Is that not? (June 9, 1969, Bhaktivedanta *VedaBase* 2003.1)

Yet many Indian Hindus continued to take *darshan* of the deities at ISKCON temples because there were few established Hindu temples in the United States and Canada when significant immigration from South Asia began in the 1960s (Eck 2000: 18; Williams 1988: 132).

Official ISKCON recognition of its Indian Hindu supporters dates to the mid-1970s when ISKCON faced ongoing attacks from the anti-cult movement in America and elsewhere. To deflect claims that ISKCON was a dangerous cult, ISKCON authorities called on its Indian supporters to authenticate ISKCON as a legitimate Hindu religious group. Thereafter, the leadership sought publicly to align ISKCON with the Hindu tradition and with its American Hindu supporters (Rochford 1985: 270). The movement formally introduced the "Life Member Programme" worldwide to ally itself with its Indian supporters. Life Members contributed moral and financial support and their membership provided ISKCON with added

---

16 As Dr. Best points out, some countries where ISKCON exists have very small or nonexistent Indian immigrant populations. In these latter locations, adaptations to decline were necessarily different. To cite one example, in Poland, approximately 2000 Indians reside in the country, most of whom are on temporary work visas. Without an alternative constituent-base to help bankroll its communities, ISKCON was forced to close temple communities in Gdansk, Krakow, Poznan, Lublin, Kielce, and Szczecin in the face of deepening financial problems and the absence of committed temple-based devotees (Rochford 2011a). Consolidation became the only viable response to decline in the absence of Indian Hindus who could be persuaded to worship at an ISKCON temple.

legitimacy. In return Indians gained authorised access to ISKCON temples to worship and to socialise with other immigrant families. By the late 1970s the Sunday feast, once an occasion for preaching and recruitment, was essentially handed over to emerging Indian Hindu congregations in locations having substantial immigrant populations in North America. However, relatively few Indians became full-time members or accepted positions of organisational responsibility. Given the growing importance of its Indian Hindu supporters, in 1980 ISKCON's GBC declared its intention to alter the public image of ISKCON from that of a "cult" to "a denomination of the Hindu church" (Rochford 1985: 271).

As ISKCON's financial problems grew to crisis levels in the mid-1980s, ISKCON's Indian Hindu supporters took on renewed importance. ISKCON leaders in North America and in Western Europe initiated a campaign to expand the Indian congregation in hopes of bringing economic stability to its beleaguered communities. The ISKCON Foundation was established in 1991 with the mission of raising funds in support of ISKCON's temple communities. The Foundation helped establish advisory boards in most of ISKCON's U.S. communities, and influential Indians comprised the majority membership of these boards. As a consequence, local Indian congregations were better positioned to exert their influence, a situation that produced tension and occasional conflict with Western devotees about the temple's purpose and about ISKCON's broader mission as a religious movement (Zaidman 1997, 2000).

The 1996 North American Prabhupada Centennial Survey allows for a comparison of the religious orientations and patterns of ISKCON involvement for 106 Indian Hindus and 318 other ISKCON members (see Rochford 2007a: 227, appendix 2, table A, 3). Indian Hindus expressed less commitment to ISKCON's religious beliefs, the movement's preaching mission, and to the authority of Prabhupada's scriptural commentaries. With respect to religious practice, Indian Hindus participated far less often in ISKCON's collective religious practices, were less likely to adhere to the four regulative principles (no meat, intoxication, illicit sex, or gambling), and to chant daily rounds. Although about equally committed as other members to the authority of the GBC and ISKCON's gurus, Indian Hindus were less committed to ISKCON's purposes and goals. Lastly, Indian Hindus contributed far fewer hours of volunteer work in their local temple community and placed less value on devotee relationships than did other ISKCON members (Rochford 2007a: 189).

In essence, the Indian Hindus affiliated with ISKCON in most cases do not share the movement's Vaishnava religious orientation and are less committed to ISKCON and the broader devotee community.

Representative of this is that one-quarter of the Indians taking part in the North American Prabhupada Centennial Survey indicated that they were not ISKCON members, despite worshiping in an ISKCON temple. These findings reveal that ISKCON's North American temples consist of two largely distinct and parallel communities. The first is made up of mostly Western converts dedicated to Prabhupada's religious teachings and vision for ISKCON; the second group is of Indian Hindus who largely see ISKCON's communities as places of worship and ethnic identification.[17] This phenomenon of parallel congregations with distinct religious and social agendas has also been noted for other immigrant religions such as Theravada Buddhism. Numrich (1996: 72-76) found striking differences between Asian immigrants and American converts in Chicago and Los Angeles with respect to religious behaviour and attitude. Although the two congregations intersected at times, interaction between them was minimal.[18]

The growing importance of Indian Hindus within ISKCON has led to unintended consequences for the movement's traditional religious culture. Because Hindus immigrating to the West come from different regions, language groups, and sects practicing diverse rituals, Hinduism is practiced as an ethnic religion outside of India (Zaidman 1997: 339). The Indian Hindus attracted to ISKCON are no different in this regard than other Hindu immigrants (Zaidman 2000: 211). However, ISKCON temples are neither dedicated to "ethnic Hinduism," nor to an eclectic form of Hinduism. ISKCON temples, for example, have traditionally been dedicated exclusively to the worship of Krishna and his incarnations. Although Indian immigrants are clearly familiar with the forms of worship, teachings, and religious practices associated with Krishna, most do not consider Krishna the supreme God (Zaidman 1997: 340). Rather they

---

17 Pyong Gap Min (2005: 107-09) argues that visiting temples helps Indian Hindu immigrants to maintain their cultural traditions and ethnic identities because of the direct connection between the Hindu religion and Indian cultural and sub-cultural traditions. The architecture of the temple, its interior furnishings, and the other visual features of the temple are all representations of Indian culture. Moreover, an Indian cultural and ethnic identity is reinforced by temple-based celebrations of major Hindu holidays, the performance of Hindu rituals, as well as by various cultural events and programming.

18 A researcher of ISKCON's Philadelphia temple during the early 1990s found that 40% of the temple residents reported that they had no relationship with Indian visitors on Sunday other than to acknowledge them by saying, "Hare Krishna." 60%, including some devotees in the temple hierarchy, admitted to holding highly critical views of the Indians (Zaidman 2000: 215). In recognition of these differences, a number of ISKCON communities worldwide hold separate Sunday feasts for Indian Hindus and for non-Indian devotees.

favour worshipping a variety of Hindu gods and acknowledge different Hindu traditions as equally valid (Zaidman 1997: 340). These differences have become points of contention as Indians have gained increasing influence within ISKCON temples.

On several occasions, festivals held at ISKCON's Spanish Fork temple in Utah were criticised by ISKCON members concerned that these events unduly catered to the Hindu community at the expense of ISKCON's religious beliefs. Beginning in 2004, the Spanish Fork temple celebrated Shiva Ratri, complete with storytelling and a sacred bathing ceremony for Lord Shiva. Included in the celebration was the chanting of Shiva's 108 names (Caru Das 2004). One devotee critic complained that "the only mention of Kr[i]s[h]na's name is that the celebration is to take place in a Kr[i]s[h]na temple. In some places the article [advertisement] comes very close to pronouncing Lord S[h]iva to be the Supreme Lord" (Hare Krsna Dasi 2004).

The influence of Indian Hindu congregations on ISKCON's religious culture can also be seen in the building of a new ISKCON temple near San Diego, California. The Indian congregation raised millions of dollars in support of the project. Plans for the temple, however, failed to strictly conform to ISKCON traditions, as they included images of Shiva and Ganesh, with accompanying samskaras and pujas "performed regularly for the Indian community" (Ragaputra Das 2005). One member of the San Diego temple community claimed that such a concession represented "kowtowing to the material conceptions of the Indian community." He added, "It's not about getting the money [from Indian supporters]; it's about serving Krishna. Better to keep the purity and remain poor, than deviate and get millions of dollars" (Ragaputra Das 2005).

Preaching has been a defining element of ISKCON's religious culture. Yet as Western devotees moved away from ISKCON's temple communities, and Indian Hindus became the primary supporters of local temples, preaching no longer represented an organisational priority. As an Indian congregational member from Bhaktivedanta Manor stated:

> Srila Prabhupada wanted the help of the Indian community no doubt but he didn't want the preaching to Westerners [to] stagnate or [be] directed entirely towards the Hindus…There is no immediate need any more to distribute books as the temples are secure because of donations from the Hindu community…Hardly any [Western] devotees are being made either. (Patel 2006)

As he comments further, the effect of the financial contributions from the Indian Hindu community is that "ISKCON's core values are watered down and are in danger of getting lost altogether. In not more than one generation much will have disappeared" (Patel 2006).

Although the ongoing Hinduisation of ISKCON represents a threat to Prabhupada's vision for ISKCON, it must also be acknowledged, as Dr. Best points out, that some Indian Hindus are becoming "ISKCONised;" that is, they accept Prabhupada's teachings and are committed to ISKCON (see e.g., Vande Berg and Kniss 2008).[19] This is because in some ISKCON communities the leadership has more consistently preached Prabhupada's teachings to the Indian congregation (see Rochford 2007a: 198-200). In addition, Pandava Sena groups for Hindu youths have also helped socialise a new generation to Prabhupada's Krishna Consciousness. And, as Dr. King and some other contributors to this volume have noted, ISKCON's Hindu members have brought substantial political and social capital to ISKCON, allowing the movement to have greater influence within mainstream society. For example, Britain's first state-funded Hindu primary school located in Harrow is aligned with ISKCON and the faith elements taught at the school are based on Prabhupada's teachings (Smullen 2011).

ISKCON's Indian Hindu congregation has clearly helped rescue a failing religious organisation. Yet, in my own view, this has come at some cost. In pursuit of needed financial resources, Prabhupada's movement has steadily advanced toward becoming a Western sect of Hinduism. Today ISKCON provides temples, leadership, and religious specialists for a sizable number of Indian Hindus throughout much of the West. In so doing, however, ISKCON has progressively aligned itself with the religious orientations of its Indian supporters and negotiated away elements of its traditional religious culture. As this has occurred, ISKCON's temple communities have become sources of estrangement for many non-Indian devotees (Rochford 2007a: 200). In sum, the threat posed by the Indian Hindu revival occurring within ISKCON is that Prabhupada's vision and teachings may be diluted, or perhaps even lost, to the organisation he founded to promote Krishna Consciousness worldwide.

---

19 Vande Berg and Kniss (2008) demonstrate that coming to accept Krishna as supreme and superior to other Hindu gods is critical to Indian immigrants becoming ISKCON devotees. Given the religious backgrounds of most Hindus immigrating to America, this represents a significant transformation in belief and one that most are unwilling to make.

Conclusion

Like any new religion, ISKCON has undergone significant change over the course of its 46 year history. The movement has certainly endured its share of controversies and large numbers of devotees have left or become marginal to ISKCON as a result. But as one devotee commented, "Leaving ISKCON does not mean leaving Krishna and Prabhupada" (Rochford 2007a: 161). Such a statement reveals the depth of spiritual commitment and understanding that Prabhupada and his successors have transmitted to their disciples and followers. Faith lives on even as Krishna Consciousness spills beyond the institutional boundaries of ISKCON.

As ISKCON's economic fortunes turned sour in the 1980s and 1990s and devotees were pushed outside the "sacred fortress" (Squarcini 2000: 256) of ISKCON's temple communities, the leadership faced the task of reinventing the organisation in order to ensure its survival into the future. Rather than continuing to vigorously preach and recruit young people, ISKCON underwent a process of goal displacement in order to stabilise the organisation and its temples. Setting aside the movement's more radical objectives, ISKCON leaders and members alike began a process of alignment with mainstream cultures. Householders found jobs in the outside labour market and children began attending state-supported schools in ever larger numbers. ISKCON leaders formed alliances with other religious groups and the movement stepped up its efforts to feed the poor throughout much of the world. To bankroll its temples, ISKCON leaders reached out to the Indian Hindu immigrant community, a move that brought both financial health and increased legitimacy to the movement. Organisational maintenance thereafter became the primary concern and Indian Hindus the focus of much of ISKCON's organisational activity. This, in turn, produced more apathy among many of ISKCON's traditional members and further curtailed efforts to preach and recruit among non-Indian people. Weakened by controversy, the leadership became more conservative in its approach and viewed the continued pursuit of ISKCON's more radical and far-reaching goals as a threat to the institutional security gained by attracting a large Indian Hindu congregation.

The question now is whether ISKCON will continue on its path toward becoming a Hindu organisation or whether the leadership will again embrace Prabhupada's determination to spread Krishna Consciousness to non-Indian people in the West and worldwide. But yesterday is not today and the devotees will need to develop new approaches if they are to reach a generation of young people often unimpressed by the anti-establishment rhetoric that helped fuel the movement's growth in the 1960s and 1970s. Because the time, the place, and the circumstances have all changed, the devotees must adapt if the movement is to attract a new generation of converts. But adaptation must not mean compromise of the movement's core teachings in the interest of short-term gains. For as every devotee knows, Prabhupada's teachings are the life and substance of Krishna Consciousness and the very basis of ISKCON's success as a religious organisation.

Bibliography

Ammerman, Nancy Tatom (1995) *Baptist Battles: Social Change and Religious Conflict in the Southern Baptist Convention.* New Brunswick: Rutgers University Press.

Amsterdam, Peter (2004) The Family—Restructuring and Renewal: An Overview of Organizational Changes—1994-2006. Paper presented at the CESNUR International Conference, Waco, Texas.

Barker, Eileen (1995) The Unification Church, in Timothy Miller (Ed.) *America's Alternative Religions.* New York: State University of New York Press, pp. 223-29.

(2004) Perspective: What Are We Studying? A Sociological Case for Keeping the "Nova." *Nova Religio* 8(1):88-102.

Bellah, Robert (1976) New Religious Consciousness and the Crisis of Modernity, in Charles Glock and Robert Bellah (Eds.) *The New Religious Consciousness.* Berkeley: University of California Press, pp. 333-52.

Bhaktivedanta *VedaBase* 2003.1. Published by the Bhaktivedanta Archives. Sandy Ridge: The Bhaktivedanta Book Trust International.

Caru, Das (2004) Shiva Ratri, the Night of Lord Shiva." *Chakra* website, February 1. www.chakra.org/announcements/eventsFeb01_04.html.

Chancellor, James (2000) *Life in the Family: An Oral History of the Children of God.* New York: Syracuse University Press.

Coward, Harold (2000) Hinduism in Canada, in Harold Coward, John Hinnells, and Raymond Williams (Eds.) *The South Asian Religious Diaspora in Britain, Canada, and the United States.* New York: State University of New York Press, pp. 151-72.

Dawson, Lorne (2002) Crises of Charismatic Legitimacy and Violent Behavior in New Religious Movements, in David Bromley and J. Gordon Melton (Eds.) *Cults, Religion and Violence.* New York: Cambridge University Press, pp. 80-101.

Desai, Krishnakant (1996) *The Final Order: The Legal, Philosophical and Documentary Evidence Supporting Srila Prabhupada's Rightful Position as ISKCON's Initiating Guru.* Bangalore: ISKCON Revival Movement.

Desai, Krishnakant, Sunil Awatramani, and Madhu Pandit Das (2004) The No Change in ISKCON Paradigm, in Edwin Bryant and Maria Ekstrand (Eds.) *The Hare Krishna Movement: The Postcharismatic Fate of a Religious Transplant.* New York: Columbia University Press, pp. 194-213.

Dwyer, Graham and Richard J. Cole (Eds.) (2007) *The Hare Krishna Movement: Forty Years of Chant and Change.* London and New York: IB Tauris.

Eck, Diana (2000) Negotiating Hindu Identities in America, in Harold Coward, John Hinnells, and Raymond Williams (Eds.) *The South Asian Religious Diaspora in Britain, Canada, and the United States,* New York: State University of New York Press, pp. 219-37.

Finke, Roger and Rodney Stark (1992) *The Churching of America: 1776-1990.* New Brunswick: Rutgers University Press.

Gallagher, Sally K. (2003) *Evangelical Identity and Gendered Family Life.* New Brunswick: Rutgers University Press.

Hare Krsna Dasi (2004) The Hinduization of ISKCON? *Chakra* website, February 12. www.chakra.org/discussions/IntFeb12_04.html.

Iannaccone, Laurence (1988) A Formal Model of Church and Sect. *American Journal of Sociology* 94: S241-S268.

Introvigne, Massimo (2000) *The Unification Church.* Salt Lake City, Utah: Signature Books.

Kanter, Rosabeth Moss (1968) Commitment and Social Organization: A Study of Commitment Mechanisms in Utopian Communities. *American Sociological Review* 33: 499-517.

(1972) *Commitment and Community.* Cambridge: Harvard University Press.

Kraybill, Donald (2001) *The Riddle of Amish Culture.* Baltimore: Johns Hopkins University Press.

Lewis, James R. and Sarah M. Lewis (2009) *Sacred Schisms: How Religions Divide.* New York: Cambridge University Press.

Lofland, John (1987) Social Movement Culture and the Unification Church, in David Bromley and Phillip Hammond (Eds.) *The Future of New Religious Movements,* Macon: Mercer University Press, pp. 91-108.

Lofland, John and Rodney Stark (1965) Becoming a World-Saver: A Theory of Conversion to a Deviant Perspective. *American Sociological Review* 30: 862-74.

Mauss, Armand (1994) *The Angel and the Beehive: The Mormon Struggle with Assimilation.* Urbana: University of Illinois Press.

Melton, J. Gordon (1991) Introduction: When Prophets Die: The Succession Crisis in New Religions, in Timothy Miller (Ed.) *When Prophets Die: The Postcharismatic Fate of New Religious Movements.* New York: State University of New York Press, pp. 1-12.

Mickler, Michael L. (2006) The Unification Church/Movement in the United States, in Eugene V. Gallagher and W. Michael Ashcraft (Eds.) *Introduction to New and Alternative Religions in America,* vol. 4. Westport: Greenwood Press, pp. 158-84.

Miller, Timothy (1991) *When Prophets Die: The Postcharismatic Fate of New Religious Movements.* New York: State University of New York Press.

Min, Pyong Gap (2005) Religion and the Maintenance of Ethnicity among Immigrants: A Comparison of Indian Hindus and Korean Protestants, in Karen Leonard, Alex Stepick, Manuel Vasquez, and Jennifer Holdaway (Eds.) *Immigrant Faiths: Transforming Religious Life in America.* Walnut Creek: AltaMira Press, pp. 99-122.

Numrich, Paul (1996) *Old Wisdom in the New World: Americanization in Two Immigrant Theravada Buddhist Temples.* Knoxville: The University of Tennessee Press.

Office for National Statistics (2009) Resident Population Estimates by Ethnic Groups, All Persons, Period: June 2009. www.neighbourhood.statistics. gov.uk/dissemination/LeadTableView.do?a=3&b=276743&c=london&d =13&e=13&f=27721&g=325264&i=1001x1003x1004x1005&l=1809&o=3 22&m=0&r=1&s=1308758527187&enc=1.

Patel, Urvashi (2006) The Need for Diversity. *Chakra* website, June 8. www. chakra.org/discussions/IntJun08_06.html.

Ragaputra Das (2005) The Hindufication of ISKCON. *Chakra* website, March 31. www.chakra.org/discussions/IntMar31_05.html.

Ravindra Svarupa Das (1994) Cleaning House and Cleaning Hearts: Reform and Renewal in ISKCON. *ISKCON Communications Journal*, two-part essay, 3: 43-52 and 4:25-33.

Rochford, E. Burke., Jr. (1985) *Hare Krishna in America*. New Brunswick: Rutgers University Press.

(1989) Factionalism, Group Defection, and Schism in the Hare Krishna Movement. *Journal for the Scientific Study of Religion* 28(2):162-79.

(1992) On the Politics of Member Validation: Taking Findings Back to Hare Krishna, in Gale Miller and James Holstein (Eds.) *Perspectives on Social Problems*, vol. 3, Greenwich: JAI Press, pp. 99-116.

(1995) Family Structure, Commitment and Involvement in the Hare Krishna Movement. *Sociology of Religion* 56(2):153-75.

(1998) Reactions of Hare Krishna Devotees to Scandals of Leaders' Misconduct, in Anson Shupe (Ed.) *Wolves within the Fold*. New Brunswick: Rutgers University Press, pp. 101-17.

(1999) Prabhupada Centennial Survey: A Summary of the Final Report. *ISKCON Communications Journal* 7(1). content.iskcon.org/icj/7_1/71rochford.html.

(2000) Demons, Karmies, and Non-devotees: Culture, Group Boundaries, and the Development of Hare Krishna in North America and Europe. *Social Compass* 47 (2): 169-86.

(2001a) Accounting for Child Abuse in the Hare Krishna: Ethnographic Dilemmas and Reflections, in David G. Bromley and Lewis Carter (Eds.) *Toward Reflexive Ethnography: Participating, Observing, Narrating*. Oxford: Elsevier Science, pp. 157-80.

(2001b) The Changing Face of ISKCON: Family, Congregationalism and Privatization. *ISKCON Communications Journal* 9: 1-12.

(2007) *Hare Krishna Transformed*. New York: New York University Press.
(2007b) Social Building Blocks of New Religious Movements: Organization

and Leadership, in David Bromley (Ed.) *Teaching New Religious Movements*. New York: Oxford University Press, pp. 159-185.

(2009) Succession, Religious Switching, and Schism in the Hare Krishna Movement, in James Lewis and Sarah Lewis (Eds.) *Sacred Schisms*. New York: Cambridge University Press, pp. 265-286.

(2011a) Preface, *Ruchi Hare Kryszna Przeobrazenia* (*Hare Krishna Transformed* in Polish). Translated by Albert Rubacha. Warsaw: Purana Publishing.

(2011b) Knocking on Heaven's Door: Charisma, Violence and the Transformation of New Vrindaban, in James Lewis (Ed.) *Violence and New Religious Movements*. New York: Oxford University Press, pp. 275-92.

Rochford, E. Burke, Jr. and Kendra Bailey (2006) Almost Heaven: Leadership, Decline and the Transformation of New Vrindaban. *Nova Religio* 9(3): 6-23.

Rochford, E. Burke, Jr. and Henry Doktorski (forthcoming) Guru Authority, Religious Innovation and the Decline of New Vrindaban, in Ann Gleig and Lola Williamson (Eds.) *Homegrown Gurus: From Hinduism in America to American Hinduism*. New York: State University of New York Press.

Shepherd, Gordon and Gary Shepherd (2002) The Family in Transition: The Moral Career of a New Religious Movement. Paper presented at the CESNUR International Conference, Salt Lake and Provo, Utah.

(2006) The Social Construction of Prophecy in The Family International. *Nova Religio* 10 (2): 29-56.

Snow, David and Cynthia Phillips (1980) The Lofland-Stark Conversion Model: A Critical Reassessment. *Social Problems* 27: 430-47.

Smullen, Madhava (2011) Krishna Avanti Plans Total of Five Schools in Coming Years. *ISKCON News*. (June 10) news.iskcon.com/node/3696.

Squarcini, Federico (2000) In Search of Identity within the Hare Krishna Movement: Memory, Oblivion, and Thought Style. *Social Compass* 47 (2): 253-71.

Squarcini, Federico and Eugenio Fizzotti (2004) *Hare Krishna*. Salt Lake City: Signature Books.

Stark, Rodney (1987) How New Religions Succeed: A Theoretical Model, in David Bromley and Phillip Hammond, *The Future of New Religious Movements*, Macon: Mercer University Press, pp. 11-29.

(1996) Why Religious Movements Succeed or Fail: A Revised General Model. *Journal of Contemporary Religion* 11 (2): 133-46.

Stark, Rodney and Roger Finke (2000) *Acts of Faith: Explaining the Human Side of Religion*. Berkeley: University of California Press.

Vande Berg, Travis and Fred Kniss (2008) ISKCON and Immigrants: The Rise, Decline, and Rise Again of a New Religious Movement. *Sociological Quarterly* 49 (1): 79-104.Wallis, Roy (1984) *The Elementary Forms of the New Religious Life*. London: Routledge and Kegan Paul.

Weber, Max (1978) *Economy and Society*, vol. 1, Guenther Roth and Claus Wittich (Eds.). Berkeley: University of California Press.

Williams, Raymond (1988) *Religions of Immigrants from India and Pakistan*. Cambridge, UK: Cambridge University Press.

Wilson, Bryan (1987) Factors in the Failure of the New Religious Movements, in David Bromley and Phillip Hammond (Eds.) *The Future of New Religious Movements*. Macon: Mercer University Press, pp. 30-45.

Yearbook of Immigration Statistics (2004) Immigration by Region and Selected Country of Last Residence: Fiscal Years 1820-2004. uscis.gov/graphics/shared/statistics/yearbook/2004/table2.xls.

Zaidman, Nurit (1997) When the Deities are Asleep: Processes of Change in an America Hare Krishna Temple. *Journal of Contemporary Religion* 12 (3): 335-52.

(2000) The Integration of Indian Immigrants to Temples Run by North Americans. *Social Compass* 47 (2): 205-19.

2. Interview with Dr Anna S. King

First Encounter

I trained as a social anthropologist in the Department of Social and Cultural Anthropology at Oxford, and studied Hindi at Cambridge before going out to do fieldwork in North India. My initial experience of Hinduism was almost entirely a South Asian one. I didn't come into contact with ISKCON devotees at that time. In fact the *pandits* and *sadhus* with whom I lived in India characterised all these followers and movements as jumped-up religions with globe-trotting gurus. So I had quite a negative understanding of ISKCON devotees as hippies who weren't particularly serious, although I did become very interested in the ways in which ideas and practices were being disseminated from India to Europe and America.

When I began to teach Religious Studies in the Education Department at Cambridge University, Bhaktivedanta Manor was accessible and extremely hospitable; so it was natural to take groups of graduate students there. The teaching of Religious Studies at the time was undergoing great change and was very exciting. Interest in contemporary and so-called new religions was at its height and there was pedagogically a realisation that textual study alone leads to a very skewed and incomplete picture of living faith communities.

We couldn't take our students to India but we could take them to Watford. They absolutely loved going to Bhaktivedanta Manor where they were cherished and welcomed, and where they could find all kinds of resources and *puja* items. Indriyesha Das and his team were exceptionally supportive and helpful, and in those days there were no fixed charges.[1] Visitors were simply asked to give a donation. These visits continued when I moved to Winchester as senior lecturer and then head of department. As a very small department we decided to focus on contemporary expressions and experiences of religion, and to encourage our students to

---

1   ISKCON Educational Services (IES) was established in 1990 at Bhaktivedanta Manor and is currently run by Indriyesha Das (Ian Andrew). Indriyesha Das and his team host events for students from various universities. Schoolchildren also come to the Manor. Most visits in fact are from primary schools, enabling children to learn about Hinduism. IES at the Manor reaches about 18,000 children annually (and includes external school visits). For more information visit www.ies.iskcon.com.

go out into the community and to get to know people from very different cultural and religious backgrounds.

When I arrived in Winchester I was asked to teach modules not only on Hinduism but on New Religious Movements, a term quite rightly disliked by ISKCON. This brought me into contact with Eileen Barker and INFORM (The Information Network on Religious Movements),[2] and with scholars studying groups in the UK like The Family, the then Unification Church, Bhagwan Rajneesh/Osho. I became involved in what Professor Eileen Barker was doing and went to conferences at the LSE—the London School of Economics. There were usually representatives of ISKCON at the LSE conferences, and I became interested in the academic study of ISKCON. The community of *brahmanas* and traditional *sannyasi*s I lived with in India had been very suspicious of, and scathing about, all the new, entrepreneurial guru movements; so it was a big jump for me to immerse myself in Vaishnava theology.

In Hardwar and Rishikesh, disciples of Maharishi Mahesh Yogi (guru of the Transcendental Mediatation movement) and the young Guru Maharaj (a leader of the Divine Light Mission) used to arrive by jumbo jet, and there was great local debate about the luxurious facilities they enjoyed. The discipline of ISKCON "hippies" and their commitment to *vaidhi-bhakti-sadhana* (devotional service) became apparent only over time. Gradually I learned to know and feel great affection for the ISKCON devotees. Now whenever I travel I seek out ISKCON temples and feel a great sense of homecoming and safety.

In 2009 I visited Kathmandu and Bali for research purposes and was delighted to meet ISKCON devotees, some under great pressure. I relax when I smell the lingering incense and polish that is so characteristic of ISKCON temples and bookstalls. This is perhaps surprising, as in the early days of the movement and even today, ISKCON has provoked violent reactions and is itself still no stranger to internal controversy and schism. It is true that right from the very beginning an almost symbiotic relationship developed between devotees and scholars. Members of ISKCON opened their movement up to researchers in a way that few other movements did. I found the polarising insider/outsider debate in Religious Studies to be misleading. Devotees, however surrendered their consciousness, do ponder reflexively upon ISKCON's theology and institutional structures.

---

2   INFORM is an independent charity founded in 1988 by Professor Eileen Barker at the London School of Economics. Its main purpose is to provide information in a balanced and up-to-date way about new or alternative religious movements and regularly holds conferences attended by religious studies experts, academics and representatives of different faith communities. For more details visit www.inform.ac.

And of course devotees believe that scholars who enter the sacred space of the temple and experience *darshan* are already receiving the grace of Krishna, and in writing about ISKCON it is held that they are also furthering the mission.

Changes, Developments and Future Prospects

The changes in ISKCON are so vast. ISKCON has developed from a small, intimate community of disciples dependent on a charismatic guru into a complex world-wide institution with an international following. There has been amazing expansion into Eastern Europe, particularly Russia and Hungary, into China and Japan, the Middle East, Central and South America, and Africa. In India, most visibly in Vrindavan and Mayapur, ISKCON is flourishing. ISKCON's Krishna Balaram temple and the marble *samadhi*—place of burial—of Prabhupada attract thousands of pilgrims each day, while in Delhi, Mumbai and other centres the continuing influence of Prabhupada's piety, mood and insistence on high standards of temple worship attracts vast congregations. At ISKCON centres one can meet devotees from Hungary, Poland, Finland and Russia, Africa, Australia, Israel, Chile, Mexico and even China and Japan. Gurus and members of the GBC are no longer predominantly Anglo-Saxon.

With the expansion of the movement there has been a growing institutionalisation and internal specialisation of function. The movement has transformed from a temple-based community to one that is increasingly congregational and family-centred. There has been an Indianisation of ISKCON, and from a society often isolated and suspicious of the outside world it has become one which is embedded in mainstream society. The postcharismatic polarisation of society into "us" and "them," devotees and non-devotees or *karmies*, is almost a thing of the past, though one can still often hear the spiritual culture of ISKCON compared to the materialism of the surrounding capitalist society. Language about other Hindu traditions, particularly the *mayavadins* or "impersonalists," is more moderate.

On the whole devotees are much better educated in devotional practice, and more knowledgeable both about Hindu culture in general and the entire tradition of Gaudiya Vaishnavism in particular. There are growing numbers of devotee-scholars and theologians, and what might be called *karmakandis* or ritual specialists. Sanskritists and Bengali speakers are continuing to expand the range of devotional materials available to devotees, and there are now institutes of higher education and theological seminaries which encourage scholarly and ritual excellence. There has been also at the top a self-conscious and reflexive examination of past mistakes and failures, and in particular of the crises of leadership. Prabhupada's own example and the presence of his pioneer disciples continue to inspire the devotees. There is some nostalgia for the austerities, commitment and clarity of purpose which accompanied the birth of the Vaishnava *bhakti* movement in the West. Prabhupada set out on a mission to re-spiritualise the world and engage in a campaign of cultural conquest, as indicated by William Deadwyler.[3] His young initiated disciples, having got high on Krishna, were then sent off, consciousness-expanded, into the unknown to set up temples and preach Krishna in far-flung places. Prabhupada's teachings about simple living and his grave warnings about modernity and industrialisation have greatly influenced the development of ISKCON's rural farms and communities. Although many such farms are organic and rely on ox-power, they have not succeeded in avoiding the use of tractors, ploughs and heavy machinery. And it is unlikely that, in the twenty-first century, devotees can transform a life-style which is heavily dependent on oil and electricity to one which is entirely self-sufficient and machinery-free. ISKCON devotees worldwide travel by aeroplanes and cars, and use the Internet very effectively. On the whole, devotees today accept Prabhupada's views that everything, even technology, can be used in the service of Krishna. While the early anti-modernist rhetoric still remains, it is now paradoxically voiced by many members of the congregation who see devotion and service, or *seva*, as a way to achieve material success and health for their families.

At a mundane level there have also been huge aesthetic changes in the physical appearance of Bhaktivedanta Manor and other temples. My mind goes directly to the provision of modern flush lavatories with soft toilet tissue—once scorned, but there is also the creation of bowers and gardens, landscaped cow barns, lakes and pools. Large ISKCON centres like Bhaktivedanta Manor nurture excellence in cultural performances of music, dance and drama, and there can be few organisations which can equal ISKCON's skills in managing festivals, pilgrimages and ecstatic crowds.

In ISKCON there are devotees who wish to remain aloof from inter-faith activities because Krishna alone should be worshipped. However, I believe that in a pluralist, multicultural society ISKCON is absolutely right to develop relations with other religious communities. To do otherwise

---

3 Deadwyler, W.D. (2007) Bringing the Lord's Song to a Strange Land: Srila Prabhupada's Strategy of Cultural Conquest and Its Prospects, in G. Dwyer and R. J. Cole (Eds.) *The Hare Krishna Movement: Forty Years of Chant and Change*. London and New York: IB Tauris, pp. 103-20.

would be to alienate the younger generation who have been brought up to value all activities conducive to greater understanding and peace between different faiths. Shaunaka Rishi's enunciation of the principles by which ISKCON should treat persons of other religious traditions was a landmark in ISKCON's development and very much to be welcomed.[4] While government resources are quite rightly being poured into projects that engage Muslim groups in interfaith encounters, projects initiated by members of Dharmic traditions are seldom reported in the media.

ISKCON has already developed ISKCON Resolve, a system of conflict management using trained mediators. The same strategies could be employed to support reconciliation between religious communities. The events which take place in the Indian subcontinent—the rise of the Hindu nationalist Right-wing, the conflicts between Pakistan and India, the treatment of Sri Lankan Tamils by Singhalese Buddhists, the bombings in Mumbai and atrocities in Gujarat, and so on—all create passions and tensions in Asian diasporic communities in the West. ISKCON cannot solve these conflicts but should be alert to support all initiatives designed to restore justice and peace.

Prabhupada can be interpreted in many ways. For example, on occasions he is very dismissive of other religions; and at other times he actually wants to bring humanity into one family. On issues like interfaith, you can cull from his speeches, his papers, sayings and reports that which would support both sides. But I certainly believe that Prabhupada should not be held to any one position. He speaks to different audiences at different times. From my point of view, ISKCON's interfaith activities are to be much applauded. I think it should go on, and I think that the search for peace and reconciliation is part of the spiritual endeavour and need not be seen as separate from Prabhupada's mission to bring Krishna to the world.

I actually play quite a strong part in interfaith dialogue. I belong to the Three Faiths Forum,[5] which is a forum for Abrahamic religions, and I am also very concerned with peace initiatives. We have a new centre

---

4   Shaunaka Rishi Das, of Irish origin, has been Director of the Oxford Centre for Hindu Studies (OCHS) since its inception in 1997. In 2004 he played the lead role in interfaith work that resulted in the publication of ISKCON's Interfaith Commission document, entitled *ISKCON and Interfaith: ISKCON in Relation to People of Faith in God*. Oxford: ISKCON Communications. ISKCON's five-point interfaith statement, together with remarks about ISKCON's mission, its theological approach to dialogue, and its principles, guidelines and purposes, are all outlined in this publication.

5   The Three Faiths Forum, founded in London in 1997, encourages friendship, goodwill and understanding amongst Muslims, Christians and Jews. It also facilitates dialogue, leading to action with people from other faiths, and those who do not subscribe to any religion. For more information visit www.threefaithsforum.org.uk.

here for peace and reconciliation, and one with which I am very strongly involved. And it's very obvious to me that it's Muslims who by far have the greater voice. Hindus do not play a particularly active role. So I do feel quite strongly that ISKCON in some senses here could be more active and be able to represent at least one Hindu voice, but otherwise is doing an excellent job.

ISKCON is wisely focusing much more of its attention on youth and youth groups, conscious that they are its future. When we remember the often unintentional cruelty involved in the treatment of young children and adolescents in the early *gurukulas* and the marginalising of the home and the family, we can only welcome the enlightened policies that ISKCON is now pursuing. The Pandava Sena[6] in particular seems to combine fun and service in a way that benefits young people themselves but also ISKCON and the wider society.

As far as the youth are concerned, one of the reasons ISKCON is so attractive to young people is its fostering of the arts. As indicated, it is immensely skilled at managing festivals. The *bhajans*, the music, even the dance that it encourages at the festivals, and also not forgetting the annual chariot procession through London, are very successful. What appeals to me about ISKCON is the joyfulness, although that sometimes does get lost. I do remember about the early days of ISKCON that it was a joyful movement. It is essentially a movement that is focused upon Krishna, the youthful Krishna of the *Bhagavata Purana*; and ISKCON brings colour and joy and fun and emphasis on delicious food. Its sensual aspect is very strong, and that, combined with the discipline that's imposed, makes it very attractive. In other words, there's a discipline, spontaneity and joyfulness that attracts youth.

I have some concern that at the level of primary and secondary education ISKCON is often the mouthpiece of Hinduism in SACRE[7] and educational conferences, and offers a homogenised understanding of South Asian religion and culture which is not fully representative of the range of distinctive religious traditions and the uniqueness of regional manifestations of belief and practice. Having just returned from a long

---

6   ISKCON Pandava Sena (IPS) is an organisation of young people between the ages of 15 and 25. IPS has a presence in cities across the UK and beyond and has representation in various university societies. For more information visit www.psena. com.

7   SACRE (Standing Advisory Councils on Religious Education) is responsible for advising Local Education Authorities (LEAs) in England and Wales on the teaching of Religious Education in schools, providing support to the LEAs and to Ofsted (the Office for Standards in Education) in the construction and implementation of an agreed syllabus.

visit to Tamil Nadu and Kerala with my students, I am very aware of the massively heterogeneous religious culture and history of India. There is a danger in the fact that ISKCON often asserts its own authority through the notion that many Hindus entertain beliefs and practise rituals without fully understanding them.

I am very interested in ISKCON's understanding of service and hospitality in the particular context of *prasadam* which nourishes and heals. I am fascinated by the way in which *prasadam* has grown into an international cuisine, a preaching tool, and a humanitarian enterprise. There is still debate in ISKCON as to whether it should be engaged in "mundane" charitable and welfare work, but the giving out of *prasadam*, sanctified food which has been offered to Krishna, falls into the category of preaching. Food for Life gives ISKCON wider social recognition and feeds and educates millions throughout the world. Such organisations target social problems and are relevant to the lives of many people. They engage with the concerns of contemporary society—environmental health, the war against poverty and malnutrition, the concern for education, the attempt to reduce our global footprint, and so on. I see ISKCON's humanitarian work, particularly in the provision of wholesome vegetarian food, as absolutely relevant to its sense of itself as an international missionary organisation. The pursuit of social justice and compassion cannot be seen as a deviation from Prabhupada's vision.

I am also fascinated by ISKCON's emphasis on education and training, and its increasing concern to recover traditional, "Vedic" life crisis rituals for its congregations, particularly those of marriage and death. The development of a strong pastoral dimension is, in my opinion, crucial to its continued expansion. My particular research interest now is in ISKCON's understanding of the good death in *bhakti*, its post-mortem rituals and the increasing use of Internet Websites as sites of mourning and remembrance. I believe this is enormously salient today as society struggles to find appropriate ways of dying, mourning and commemorating the dead.

The Hare Krishna movement is a global one and although its rituals, festivals and patterns of worship are universal, the movement still has to accommodate to particular cultures and political regimes. For example, the Hungarian temple and farm led by Shivaram Swami has a very different ambience or mood from that of Bhaktivedanta Manor, presided over by Srutidharma Das as Temple President, or the Chowpatty Mumbai temple and ashram developed by Radhanath Swami.[8] Each has its distinctive features. Similarly there is a growth of diversity among devotees.

8   Sivarama Swami is an ISKCON guru and member of the Governing Body Commission (GBC) responsible for leading ISKCON's mission in Hungary, Romania

Braja Bihari or Brian Bloch, an American devotee living in India, likes to classify devotees as pizzas and pakoras.[9] I don't see it quite that way but I do accept his general argument. For example, I recently met a young temple *pujari* (one who tends to the deities) in Nepal who was very literalist in his approach to scriptures, to *varnashramadharma* (caste system) and to gender, while in Vrindavan I was fortunate enough to encounter some of Prabhupada's earliest and oldest American and British disciples whose language combined the quaintness of Prabhupada's English with the counter-cultural idioms of the 1960s. Many displayed a well-developed sense of humour for the idiosyncrasies of ISKCON and a tolerance for dissent and diversity. This growth of internal diversity I see as bringing ISKCON into the mainstream of society. While it often creates major tensions, it also enriches the society, making it a broad church. I believe that in becoming an ecumenical, tolerant and healing community with many voices, ISKCON is strengthened rather than weakened.

I suspect that many older people rather miss the ardent devotees with shaven heads and saffron robes who handed out devotional literature, and danced and chanted through the main streets of our cities with their *kartals*—hand-cymbals—and *mridangas*—drums. People often ask me where they have gone. Of course they are still there, but often in Western-style clothes and engaged in other forms of mission and preaching. ISKCON is no longer seen in Europe and America as a slightly weird but harmless group of hippies who are crazy for Krishna. Devotees are out there in mainstream events—at civic receptions, interfaith meetings, humanitarian fundraising events and involved in SACRE. ISKCON, in

---

and Turkey. Within ISKCON, Sivarama Swami is also well-known for his deep knowledge of Vaishnava literature, and has written several books about Gaudiya Vaishnavism. Radhanath Swami is also an ISKCON guru, a member of ISKCON's GBC and works largely from Mumbai in India, as well as traveling extensively throughout Europe and America. He has been instrumental in the founding of the Mumbai Bhaktivedanta Hospital. Srutidharma Das is not an ISKCON guru but recently joined a GBC sub-committee, with a focus on strategy, and he was appointed to the post of temple president at Bhaktivedanta Manor in 2010. Since the early 1980s he has worked tirelessly to cultivate and encourage many Gujaratis and other members of the Indian community in London who now support Bhaktivedanta Manor with great enthusiasm.

9   In an analysis of opposing voices or perspectives in ISKCON, Braja Bihari Dasa (Brian Bloch) has developed a number of models in an attempt to find solutions to conflict. One of these models identifies two major groupings in ISKCON: (1) devotees who select and weave together ideas from a range of conservative and liberal points of view (the "pizza" group), and (2) devotees who fall into opposing conservative or liberal camps (the "pakoras"). For a full discussion of these ideas and viewpoints, see Dasa, B.B. (2005) Pizza or Pakoras: Reconciling Conservative and Liberal Viewpoints in ISKCON, *ISKCON Communications Journal* 11.

that sense, has become acculturated. The danger therefore perceived by some devotees is that there is a growth in secularisation, egalitarianism and rationalism that will be at the expense of the strict teachings of Prabhupada and his spiritual lineage.

When I first started teaching, interest in new religions was at its greatest intensity. Religious Studies as a discipline had exotic faith communities on its doorstep. There was no need to travel to India or Japan or China. Religion suddenly became newsworthy with reports of brainwashing and indoctrination. Media stories about new cults were consumed by a public which knew very little about their history. Anti-cult organisations flourished. The UK tends to be rather private in its religious life, so ISKCON devotees were often viewed as eccentrically passionate and public in their religious activities. The public was often unaware of the differences between the various so called cults—whether those of Bhagwan Rajneesh/Osho, Maharish Mahesh Yogi, Guru Maharaj, the Moonies or ISKCON. Chithurst Buddhist monks setting out to fly the flag on bindabat were mistaken for Hare Krishnas and sometimes taunted on the streets. The bobble hats, the *dhotis*, the orange robes and the strange sandalwood markings were seen as very exotic. On the other hand, ISKCON's association with the counter-culture, with the Beatles, particularly George Harrison, with Allen Ginsberg, with Top of the Pops and the chart-topping records of the *Hare Krishna Mantra* and *The Radha Krsna Temple* gave ISKCON a particularly cool image. Given the subjective turn to the East in the 1960s, the plangent notes of the sitar and drone often defined what it meant to be spiritual. For Dhananjaya Das[10] and many others, this was an exciting time to be young.

Today, ISKCON in the UK has matured. Its demographic corresponds much more closely to that of the wider population. There was great excitement and indignation when a cow was "euthanized" by the RSPCA (Royal Society for the Prevention of Cruelty to Animals) but, in general, media stories are sober reportings of the Diwali celebrations at the House of Commons or ISKCON's link to a new Hindu school in Harrow.[11]

---

10 Dhananjaya Das, of Scottish origin, is among the earliest British disciples initiated by ISKCON's Founder A.C. Bhaktivedanta Swami Prabhupada. He helped George Harrison discover the estate of Piggott's Manor, after which it was donated to ISKCON in 1973 and renamed Bhaktivedanta Manor. After running a restaurant in Vrindavan, India, and an ISKCON Temple in Amsterdam, Dhananjaya Das presently lives near Bhaktivedanta Manor.

11 The Krishna Avanti School in Harrow is the first state-funded Hindu school in Britain. ISKCON is its official faith partner. For further details about the school see www. krishna-avanti.org.uk.

Perhaps even more interesting is the change in Indian perceptions. I have already said that when I was living as a young anthropologist with a *brahmana* community in a sacred *tirtha* (holy place) in North India, ISKCON was not taken seriously. Today such attitudes have changed. The sacrifices made by the early devotees, together with ISKCON's ritual punctiliousness and humanitarian work, have gained it admiration and acceptance. The massive Food for Life international programme has been hugely important in that respect.

ISKCON has also changed such that the early devotees didn't know so much about Hinduism or indeed about Vaishnavism. Increasingly, devotees have grown in knowledge of both theology and the ritual tradition. They've understood more about the pluralism of Hinduism. Now you get Sanskritists amongst the devotees; you get ritualists, priests, and so on. There is a much more inclusive aspect to ISKCON. The suspicion of the outer world and the comparison of Vaishnava spirituality with the decadence of society are no longer there. Devotees have changed so that attitudes to all kinds of things have altered.

ISKCON has much to offer people in today's varied landscape. ISKCON has touched the lives of many people with colour, warmth and vitality. Its path—the path of ecstatic, joyful and experiential *bhakti-yoga*—strikes a chord with many people round the world who long for intimacy and community. Prabhupada taught that the very personal love between God and human beings should be reflected in the community of Vaishnavas. Godbrothers and godsisters are enjoined to care for each other and to foster and nurture each other's spiritual development. Prabhupada also brought to the West "Vedic" ideals and values of altruistic service and hospitality. He introduced festivals, including Janmashtami and the annual Ratha Yatra, ecstatic *kirtan*s and *bhajan*s, respect for culinary skills and delicious food. His teachings about vegetarianism, animal protection and simple living were in many ways prophetic as concern about global warming, environmental degradation, the provenance of food and exploitation of the Earth's resources deepens. ISKCON's influence in the UK and elsewhere has often had a ripple effect. Many people who have never visited a temple have come into indirect contact with ISKCON through its literature, its music or its teachings on cow protection or on vegetarianism.

Yet many long-term devotees and leaders are concerned that ISKCON will not be able to maintain its adherents and attract new followers. Some American temples remain empty and those in Europe often rely on the service of Polish, Russian and Hungarian devotees. There is also the concern that the second and third generations of the Indian congregation will not be as generous donors and sponsors as their parents. I suspect, like Rasamandala Das, that ISKCON will turn from hunter and gatherer to cultivator, and that it will be less concerned with the public who show an interest in Krishna Consciousness and much more concerned with the welfare of the existing community and the personal development of the individual devotee. People without a particular faith commitment but with common interests will still be drawn to ISKCON's vegetarian cooking classes, its animal husbandry or courses in Ayurveda or yoga.

I particularly welcome the stress placed by ISKCON today on training courses for core and congregational members, and on educating its young devotees to understand and take part in the intellectual debates of the society around them. I believe that this is essential if the Society is to enjoy wise leadership and to be attractive to young people in the age of the credit-crunch and an aging population.

A lot of devotees in the past were only partially informed about their own tradition and really didn't know much about the scholarly debates that were going on in other disciplines. But there is now quite a width about it that actually enriches ISKCON, and I see this as very positive. The creation of many voices or diversity is often seen by devotees as extremely problematic; but I see it as being absolutely intrinsic to the growth of any movement that wants to survive beyond the immediate postcharismatic stage of its development.

So I think that the prospects for ISKCON are good but that mission will be understood in many different ways. ISKCON is not going to conquer the world with devotion to Krishna but it will continue to grow and flourish.

Indian and Non-Indian Devotees

In the UK ISKCON has set out successfully to cultivate and attract the Hindu population of over half a million by outreach visits, Friends of Lord Krishna—FOLK—or *nama hatta* groups,[12] preaching and personal contact. I know that many white devotees fear a swamping effect, a creeping Hindu syncretism and a gradual loosening of strict adherence to Prabhupada's instructions. In the final analysis, they fear that ISKCON will become a branch of Hinduism without the early missionary zeal inspired by Prabhupada.

12 *Nama hatta* house groups were set up in the UK by Bhaktivedanta Manor's Kripamoya Dasa. These house groups were initially called Friends of Lord Krishna (FOLK), but in 1985 Kripamoya Dasa changed the name to *nama hatta*.

However, their fears may be exaggerated. Firstly, many of the congregation are Gujaratis with a particular devotion to Krishna, and secondly it is extremely doubtful whether ISKCON could survive in its present form without the generous funding and active contribution of Indian Hindus. Because many of the congregation are Gujaratis—and, therefore, have grown up with a devotion to Krishna –among them there is actually quite a great deal of diversity too. I mean some of them you meet at Bhaktivedanta Manor do have devotion to Shiva as well as to Krishna. So I feel they enlarge ISKCON's role.

Also, we only have to look at the accounts of particular temples to note the generosity of Indian patrons compared to that of non-Indian devotees who have not been brought up within a culture of donation. Increasingly, it is members of the Indian congregation who respond to training initiatives and opportunities. At Bhaktivedanta Manor Indian Hindus are often tireless in their service. On the whole, the contribution of birth Hindus has deepened understanding of *bhakti* as practised in India and given ISKCON a new role as instructor to a younger generation of Hindus. It is unlikely that ecstatic devotion to a personal God could have swept the world in the way that early devotees envisaged.

Expansion in the number of Indian Hindus also means that ISKCON gains great political and cultural recognition from society at large. In the past the Hindu community mobilised to support the Hare Krishna Temple Defence Movement formed in 1990 and joined a large scale protest march in 1994. The support of the Hindu community meant that international and national media reported the campaign, and that it became a significant news item in Hindu and Asian communities across the world. The more recent issue of cow killing by the RSPCA similarly galvanised some Hindus into active support.

The identification of ISKCON with the wider Hindu community creates influential networks and pressure groups, and enables ISKCON to actively promote some of the goals of the Society. The expanding numbers of Indian Hindus gives the leadership a more nuanced understanding of the diversity of Asian religious traditions, and on the whole engenders less rigid, more inclusive attitudes to other *sampradaya*s (traditions). The growth of the Indian Hindu congregation has also necessitated the development of a clergy trained to minister pastorally and ritually to its members, while Hindu pilgrims expect to be able to perform customary rituals such as the ceremonies of *mundan* and ear piercing.

However, there is still a long way to go before the UK's lakes and rivers are assimilated to those of Vrindavan or British temples are truly understood to be the scenes of Radha-Krishna's pastimes. There still remains to this day a tension between seeing India as the sacred land and the site of Vedic culture and embracing the idea that Krishna and Radha are physically present wherever they are worshipped.

Theological Challenges: Conservative and Liberal Perspectives

I welcome the growing diversity as part of the process of maturation which will enable ISKCON to be a hospitable home for all seekers, whether conservative or liberal. Without preserving scriptural authority a religious tradition cannot survive but neither can it survive without the flexibility to reinterpret revelation to meet new circumstances. Conservatives and liberals both cite Prabhupada's words. This is hardly surprising given the vast cumulative record of Prabhupada's writings, purports and talks. I agree with Hopkins[13] that there is a tendency in ISKCON to treat every statement made by Prabhupada as if it has *ex cathedra* authority, and that the question of the relative authority of Prabhupada's statements with regard to each other and the question of their authority in relation to Vaishnava scriptures and to other teachers within the Chaitanya tradition are serious theological questions. I am more sanguine, however, that ISKCON will become broad and inclusive, offering a refuge to all devotees who accept Krishna as ultimate Lord.

One of the major shifts is the fact that ISKCON has transmitted Krishna Consciousness all over the world and in so doing has come into contact with a great variety of cultures and religious traditions. This is not the place to detail the shifts in philosophy and theology that have resulted but I would suggest that the language used by ISKCON itself indicates some shifts. Words like "clergy," "congregation," "monks," and "nuns" are not altogether neutral. Moreover, ISKCON now has Sanskritists and theologians of distinction who have easy, online access to theological and philosophical resources unknown to scholars of the past.

ISKCON has tirelessly collated the works of Prabhupada and has commenced the process of doing the same with the writings of his predecessors. It has preserved written records of devotees and documented its own history in the West. A discussion has already begun as to how far sacred texts should be understood literally and how far ISKCON gurus can apply their own insights or those of other teachers within the Chaitanyite

---

13 Hopkins, T. J. (2007) ISKCON's Search for Self-Identity: Reflections by a Historian of Religions, in G. Dwyer and R. J. Cole (Eds.) *The Hare Krishna Movement: Forty Years of Chant and Change.* London and New York: IB Tauris, pp. 171-92.

tradition. Hopkins[14] in his work on ISKCON's search for self-identity raises the question as to whether Prabhupada's authority is absolute for all time, and how far other Vaishnava teachers can speak with authority about Krishna. This kind of theological and philosophical reflection will be unsettling and painful for many devotees but it is an inevitable process of self-discovery which can only deepen ISKCON's understanding of its own heritage and history. Without a process of continual introspection and reinterpretation, the relevance of ISKCON to mainstream society will be extinguished.

I can understand how devotees read texts in particular ways. But with the Internet, devotees are constantly rubbing up against people from different cultures with different ideas. Indeed, some of the ideas that you find among the congregation at Bhaktivedanta Manor include, for example, the idea that all knowledge is found in the Vedas, the idea that they had bombs and aircraft in the Vedas, as well as even computers being found in the Vedas. All sorts of things are said by devotees about how long humanity has lived on the Earth and about the nature of the universe, some of which is in strong disagreement with empirical, scientific understandings at present.

In order to remain relevant, ISKCON has to address the knowledge that contemporary society has. It can't just slide off; otherwise it will just become irrelevant. What will happen increasingly is that there will be closer analysis of texts, both of Prabhupada's and his predecessors'. The question of people like Radhanath Swami and Shivaram Swami and their status will also come under strong scrutiny in terms of considerations as to whether, theologically, everything stops with Prabhupada or whether new Vaishnava gurus will emerge who can deepen our understanding. Finally, it is only devotion to Krishna that really matters. But, of course, in ISKCON there are all kinds of ritual understandings, philosophical and so on. ISKCON is a *parampara*; that is to say, it does define knowledge in terms of authentic gurus. All these things are very complicated and challenging. So ISKCON will do what members of other religions have done in the past: struggle, and struggle with new ideas and so on; and from that will emerge understandings that will be relevant to the next generations.

Moving on now to the ISKCON Revival/Reform Movement, this identifies itself with the *ritvik* philosophy, and I myself receive their magazine, *Back to Prabhupada*. The tireless critique of Krishnakant Desai and the unflagging criticisms, even mockery, of the *diksha* gurus may annoy members of the GBC, but on the other hand they may act like gadflies to

14 Ibid. p. 186.

sting ISKCON into life. Today, as Radha Mohan Das has argued,[15] the autocratic powers of ISKCON initiating gurus have been curbed and the kind of excessive reverence enjoyed by past gurus has disappeared. A flatter or localised management system has replaced the old hierarchies. However, many disciples place extraordinary trust in the capacity of their guru to advise them in many aspects of life, and this does carry dangers. In India there are systems of checks and balances but elsewhere great vigilance is required, particularly where the guru has large numbers of disciples and is not aware of their individual circumstances.

Then there are figures such as Bhaktivedanta Narayana Maharaja;[16] but I have never really seen them as great threats, and of course charismatic living gurus will always attract disciples. When the Hare Krishna move-

15 Cole, R. J. (Radha Mohan Das) (2007) Forty Years of Chanting: A Study of the Hare Krishna Movement from its Foundation to the Present Day, in G. Dwyer and R. J. Cole (Eds.) The Hare Krishna Movement: Forty Years of Chant and Change. London and New York: IB Tauris, pp. 26-53.

16 Bhaktivedanta Narayana Maharaja (1921-2010) was thought to be a well-wisher of ISKCON for many years and was also a personal friend of Prabhupada. Prior to 1991, Narayana Maharaja's large following was essentially restricted to Indians outside ISKCON. However, after 1991 many of his followers were ex-ISKCON members, with the majority of his Western followers leaving ISKCON to join him in 1995. It was in this year that a major Governing Body Commission (GBC) action was taken on the matter. Following many years of tension, in April 2010 ISKCON's GBC then released a forty-page document clarifying the relationship between Prabhupada and Narayana Maharaja. This document presents a statement about a meeting held in October 2009 in Govardhana, India between Narayana Maharaja and several senior members of the GBC. During the meeting, according to the document, ISKCON leaders apologised to Narayana Maharaja for their failure to communicate with him in a proper and timely manner in 1995, making mention also of the policies that they had established concerning members of ISKCON taking instruction from non-ISKCON gurus. The document makes it clear that ISKCON's leaders, although wishing to remain on courteous terms with Narayana Maharaja, are also strongly critical of him; for, as they see it, Narayana Maharaja has persistently misrepresented ISKCON's founder-acharya by claiming that the founder entrusted Narayana Maharaja with an ongoing role in the spiritual leadership of the Krishna Consciousness movement. The ISKCON leadership rejects this claim in toto. For further details see www.news.iskcon.com/node/2657#ixzz0wl0Xg9wB. It is important to point out here that, while all these events have been significant, particularly in terms of ISKCON's developing and maturing sense of its own self-identity, Narayana Maharaja no longer remains a personal threat to ISKCON, as he passed away on 29th December 2010. However, it still remains possible that his followers or disciples will continue to unhold his teachings, which may, in turn, cause them to clash with members of ISKCON. How the relationship between disciples of Narayana Maharaja and members of ISKCON will develop in the future will have important consequences for the evolution of both groups. The two groups may in the future continue to remain separate, though there is a possibility too that they will even be united. For further discussion of Narayana Maharaja and his disciples, see the interviews with Steven Rosen and Edith Best in this volume.

ment was fledgling they could have acted to destabilise and confuse the movement, but I do not see that happening now and I think there are very positive signs of reconciliation and accommodation. Previously, ISKCON devotees were not encouraged to associate with Narayana Maharaja and many ISKCON leaders regarded him as setting out to poach devotees and to subvert Prabhupada's exclusive position within ISKCON as spiritual master. Having read some transcripts of Narayana Maharaja's *darshans* and interviews with ISKCON devotees I found some evidence for this. On several occasions Narayana Maharaja told ISKCON devotees that if they wanted pure *bhakti* they should come to him; if they wanted money they should go to ISKCON leaders who were *adama-bhakti*, the lowest class of *bhakti*.

When Narayana Maharaja was in Vrindavan some initiated devotees did align themselves with him, finding inspiration in his teachings, but other devotees—mostly young devotees—visited him secretly. Like young people everywhere they were curious and found it rather exciting to do something that was forbidden. I thought that the mature devotees treated their escapades with wisdom and humour. ISKCON is now sufficiently mature to accept that Vaishnava gurus should not necessarily be seen as rivals.

Women and Gender Roles

My interest in gender and in exploring the feminine and feminist dimensions of deity with a focus on Radha, is, I believe, very relevant. I have argued elsewhere[17] that the Chaitanyite tradition has resources for greater inclusivity which need to be explored. The position of Radha in ISKCON is seen as confidential but also ambivalent. Radha is depicted both as equal to Krishna and as hierarchically contained by Him. I would like to suggest that the love within the Godhead could be an excellent model for a thealogy of the female divine that could result in the greater recognition and incorporation of women's devotional experience. ISKCON theology reflects a male, heterosexual understanding of both the Godhead and of human nature.

There has not been a sustained feminist or queer critique of the central texts and practices of Hare Krishna devotees. In fact for most devotees—both men and women—this would reduce spiritual transcendence to the materialist platform. At a practical level there is, as one might

---

17 King, A. S. (2007) Thealogising Radha: The Feminine and Feminist Dimensions of Deity, in G. Dwyer and R. J. Cole (Eds.) *The Hare Krishna Movement: Forty Years of Chant and Change.* London and New York: IB Tauris, pp. 171-229.

imagine, considerable diversity; culture, education and regionality play a strong part in shaping expectations of gender roles. There are many women devotees who have found in ISKCON's more traditionalist attitudes towards the role of women a greater respect than they have found outside in an ostensibly egalitarian culture. They find in the idea of separation of roles and the primacy of women with regard to family and children great comfort, safety and dignity. Many women converts to Islam and Orthodox Judaism as well as conservative evangelical Christianity hold out the same arguments.

However, other women have found that these same patterns of respect mask a patriarchal control and lack of freedom. In practice many women devotees live lives very similar to those of other women in the UK—working outside the home and balancing the responsibilities of work, family and leisure. In ISKCON attitudes are often ambivalent. One can find centres, as in Hungary, which aspire to re-enact or perform the traditional "Vedic" roles of women and men, but where women have responsibility as accountants, farm workers and doctors. One can also find centres—e.g. in Alachua, Florida—where women espouse apparently feminist ideas, but who follow Prabhupada's instructions on sexual restraint within, as well as outside, marriage.

Many of the younger generation are going to universities—unlike their parents who gave up everything to follow Prabhupada—and are becoming teachers, midwives, social workers, lawyers and university lecturers. The public literature of ISKCON remains profoundly heterosexual, despite the known fact that ISKCON has had several initiating gurus who were homosexual.[18] The position of gay or transsexual men and women is still a matter of debate within ISKCON, with Prabhupada's words being quoted by both conservatives and liberals alike, but increasingly leaders are adopting the more libertarian values of the wider society.

There has been a great change in the terms of the positions of men and women in ISKCON. Prabhupada called young women and men to serve Krishna, gave formal initiation to women and employed them in a

18 No initiated member of ISKCON, let alone one who is a guru, is permitted to engage in physical expressions of homosexuality. For example, in 1989 Bhavananda Das (formally Bhavananda Goswami) was stripped of his guru status for having confessed to engaging in homosexual acts whilst operating as an ISKCON guru. However, he is currently the Creative Director of the Temple of the Vedic Planetarium project in Mayapur, ISKCON's world headquarters in West Bengal. This shows that there is some degree of tolerance and accommodation of homosexual devotees in ISKCON today. Also, in ISKCON the Gay and Lesbian Vaishnava Association provides comment and discussion on matters of homosexuality and on a variety of issues relating to sexuality. See www.galva108.org.

variety of roles. However, some of his comments about women as more emotional, infantile and in need of protection would be regarded today as extremely demeaning to women; they reveal the strength of the patriarchal tradition of the time. With the increasing influence of male ascetics or *sannyasis* in ISKCON in the postcharismatic period, married householders and women were often regarded with contempt, and women were sometimes humiliated and exploited. There was wife and child abuse.

This black period of ISKCON's history has now gone and the GBC has apologised to women.[19] Women teach classes in many temples and act as *pujaris*, and there are many who are respected for their devotion, saintliness and service throughout global ISKCON. Initiating gurus remain male, although women have served on the GBC. Women are still not permitted to take *sannyasa,* although there are *brahmacharins* or nuns vowed to celibacy. The practice of arranged marriages between devotees from sometimes very different cultures and nationalities still persists in temple communities but in a much more benign and considered form. ISKCON remains on the whole conservative in regard to matters of gender and sexuality, but different temples have different approaches. What may be easily accepted in one centre may be repudiated by another.

The leaders of ISKCON, on the one hand, will have to consider gender roles in the light of government acts, educational guidelines, legal provision for civil partnerships, and so on. All these take us towards a more inclusive egalitarian society but possibly diminish the role of spiritual authorities. The growth of congregational ISKCON will also have a great impact on how gender roles develop. In India as well as in the UK and in America, ISKCON's values will to some extent be shaped by the values and attitudes of the wider society. ISKCON will have the same kind of debates and tensions that other religious traditions have faced or are facing. There is a need to support those women who regard their primary role as being within the family and to empower those who wish to take stronger leadership roles.

Increasingly, liturgies and rituals in all religious traditions are inclusive of women's experience, including motherhood and sexuality. There has already been what could be called a feminisation of religion, with God being associated with the feminine qualities of tenderness, and religious traditions being seen as healing rather than hierarchical. Motherhood has always been seen as an essential issue of feminism, and the idealisation of motherhood can also be seen as a form of control. Being a mother is an extraordinarily important facet of women's lives, but not the only one.

19 The mistreatment of women in ISKCON was acknowledged by the GBC resolutions in 2000, and a new regime introduced.

The sanctity of motherhood should not be at odds with the dignity of womanhood. Women should be defined in terms of themselves as well in terms of the family.

Concluding Thoughts and Reflections

ISKCON has a very dominating voice in Hinduism when it comes to the representation of Hinduism nationally. I have suggested that this becomes more critical when it comes to the school curriculum. While ISKCON leaders try very hard to present a diverse understanding of the Hindu tradition, there is a homogenising tendency which sees particular Vedic texts and traditions as central and which tends to obscure the great diversity of Hindu traditions and what one might call the vernacular or popular aspects of Hinduism. Prabhupada's books are inspirational, but are in the tradition of Gaudiya Vaishnavism and involve a strict following of *parampara*, disciplic succession, and a literalist understanding of scripture.

I feel that there are two aspects of ISKCON that might be an impediment to its maturation as an inclusive and compassionate society. The first is about science. To try to replace science with a kind of religious fundamentalism, Prabhupada uses expressions such as the "science of self-realisation," "science of God," "Vedic science," and so on. In many, almost all of his writings, he pokes fun at, or ridicules, modern science as mechanistic and reductive. This hostility has been inherited and formalised by disciples like Michael Cremo and Richard Thompson[20] and by those who believe that science should become truly religious. In most of their writings they put up straw men which they then knock down; but the arguments are really out of date. Many devotees I have met show hostility to science, but they are very ignorant of what science is, namely, an empirical discipline that tests hypotheses.

Bhakti Svarupa Damodara Swami,[21] who set up the Bhativedanta Institute, describes himself as a scientist working at the interface of

20 Michael Cremo (Drutakarma Dasa) and Richard Thompson (Sadaputa Dasa) are American disciples of Bhaktivedanta Swami Prabhupada who co-authored a controversial book: Cremo, M. A. and R. L. Thompson (1993) *Forbidden Archeology: The Hidden History of the Human Race.* Los Angeles: Bhaktivedanta Book Publishing. They argue in their book that modern humans have lived on the Earth for billions of years, and their work has attracted attention from Hindu creationists and paranormalists, but have been labelled as pseudoscience by representatives of the mainstream archaelogical and paleoanthroplogical communities.

21 Bhakti Svarupa Damodara Swami (1937-2006)—also known as Dr Thoudam Damodara Singh—was an ISKCON guru, writer and poet. For more than 30 years he was the International Director of the Bhaktivedanta Institute, promoting the study of the relationship between science and Vedanta. Within ISKCON, Bhakti Svarupa

science and religion. What he is really trying to do is persuade scientists of the scientific value of religion, particularly Vaishnavism. I feel that devotees in this respect are being led down wrong paths.

Prabhupada sees science in a way as devoid of spiritual value. These kinds of debate were being held in the nineteenth century in the West, and they are being re-run. I actually do enjoy reading a lot of the ISKCON literature, but it isn't properly empirical; it doesn't really look at, for example, what archaeologists are saying. It takes records from the past, but it is quite spurious in many ways. I do understand that what Prabhupada is saying is that knowledge is not just what you find in a laboratory; there are spiritual disciplines, and so on; and that science shouldn't be the death of God, if you like. But there are different ways of tackling the relationship between science and religion that, in the end, are more valuable. The kind of arguments that ISKCON persists in having are antediluvian.

These arguments are being re-run because Prabhupada was hostile to the idea that life comes from life. He put great stress on the Creator. He was hostile to evolution,[22] and his disciples have inherited an opposition to it. Also, since they often take a literal stance to scripture, there is an assumption that humans have lived on the earth for millions and billions of years, far beyond that which scientists claim is factually discoverable. The idea that the cosmos has regenerated itself through millennia, and that human beings have lived through cycles of lives, do seem to be at odds with the tentative conclusions of modern science.

I would see a much more fruitful approach to be, for example, emphasising the idea that science could be seen as the revelation of Krishna. Indeed, I think that the kind of disputes in Christianity that have been played out mean that many modern physicists, who are Christians, would hold and understand evolution to be, in a sense, a divine revelation. There are more helpful ways such as have been pursued by Christian physicists that ISKCON could think about in relation to these topics. In other words, science can be seen as a spiritual exploration. But in seeing it as a competitor, ISKCON devalues itself. If indeed Krishna is Ultimate Creator, then science is part of that creation, and it should be valued as such.

I lived in a very poor part of India, where children died very often at birth, where water was polluted, where there was great poverty. So the

---

Damodara Swami was seen as a pioneer involved in advancing the dialogue towards a synthesis of science and spirituality throughout the world.

22 ISKCON's continued opposition to the theory of evolution is especially prominent in terms of arguments about the origin of humans and other life-forms. In ISKCON, emphasis is placed on the teaching that humans are the offspring of demigods, celestial beings called the Manus, and therefore have not evolved from lower species or from other life forms; see *Bhagavad Gita As it Is*, 10.6. Purport.

input of science in a sense—making sure that the umbilical cord is treated in a way to minimise infection, and so on—is crucial, enabling people to flourish. Actually, what is so odd is that ISKCON uses science all the time. As I have already indicated, even on its organic farms you find computers; and, even though there is ox power, you can also see tractors and heavy machinery in the background. Devotees fly and Prabhupada also flew in aeroplanes. And when Prabhupada was ill I know that he tried lots of spiritual remedies; but there were occasions when he resorted to hospital, scientific-based treatment, too.

When Prabhupada came his mission was to arouse spirituality, to arouse Krishna Consciousness. He saw himself as being in a secular, scientific, mechanistic world, which had no place for spiritual values. So I can really empathise with that, and I do understand that ISKCON's mission is to reflect it. I know ISKCON devotees who look at, say, the *Bhagavata Purana* and other scriptures, see them as giving correct information about the world: Prabhupada and the Moon, for example.[23] Of course, as an anthropologist I listen carefully; but they are stuck in a restricted mode of comprehension. The literature of ISKCON—what is sold in its bookshops—presents a hostile face to science; and I would want to argue that this is a danger.

The second and final point that I want to make is about the nostalgia for *varnashramadharma* some devotees have; that is to say, their nostalgia for a society based on this. Swami Prabhupada states clearly in many commentaries that he wishes to re-establish the ancient Vedic system of *varnashramadharma*, the division of human society into four spiritual and occupational orders.[24] I have just returned from visiting South India and believe that whatever the virtues such a social system may possess,

---

23 Bhaktivedanta Swami Prabhupada often stated that astronauts have never actually visited the Moon, claiming the attempt of scientists to reach the moon would not be possible because it would be barred by god Indra (*Srimad Bhagavatam*, 5.24.3 purport). He has also commented (see *Srimad Bhagavatam*, 6.4.6 purport and *Srimad Bhagavatam*, 8.5.34 purport) that since the Moon-god is the presiding deity of vegetation on the Moon, plants would be found there, yet scientists hold that it is a barren desert. Thus, in Prabhupada's view, astronauts could not possibly have gone there.

24 From ISKCON's perspective, the concept of *varna* must be sharply distinguished from what is found in the traditional caste system of India. In ISKCON, the whole system of caste in India today is considered to be debased and emphasis is placed upon an individual's personal spiritual aspirations and qualities rather than insisting on birthright as the determinant of religious status or practice. Thus, for example, to receive initiation into the *brahmana* or priestly office in ISKCON, there is no barrier to this based on social standing in contradistinction to what is seen in the caste system. Nevertheless, the hierarchical logic of caste does indeed have its origins in India's ancient socio-religious system known as *varnashramadharma*.

theoretically, in terms of stability and harmony, its effects still continue in the exploitation and oppression of millions of people. While devotees emphasise that they would espouse the authentic Vedic system in which innate qualities determine *varna*, this still remains for me an ill-judged conception.

All this comes out of my work with *dalits* (casteless people) over many years. The nostalgia that some devotees express to try to reintroduce *varnashramadharma* is extremely complex. Prabhupada wanted to create a *brahman*ical order that would be the head of society. But, if it were possible to recreate it at all, this can be oppressive. Devotees can seem to me to try to create a hierarchical society in which *dalits* themselves do not feel at home, do not feel comfortable. The reality is that still in Tamil Nadu, for example, millions of people are marrying within caste; they are still doing jobs that are at the lower end of occupation. I am always surprised that in this "new" India, which is so affluent and so vigorous and dynamic, that next to the advanced genetics laboratory there are still people living with sewage coming into their homes.

I would argue that in any modern, complex society any attempt to reintroduce any form of *varnashramadharma* would be almost impossible. Moreover, the idea that you could recreate a rural scenario, with a potter here and a *brahmana* there, and that they will be egalitarian, is a dream. It's a dream. And devotees who seek to reintroduce it—I know they never would—should see the reality of what actually happens; and they should see the injustices that many people in India suffer. There are horrendous incidents every week for women who have been described as the *dalits* of *dalits*. I think, too, that we should remember how the police, the law courts, and so on, treat people who have no real stake in society and the abuses that are carried on. ISKCON organisations in Vrindavan and places like that are doing a lot to ease the plight of the poor; but it's not enough. It's not nearly enough. Those idealists who assume that *varna* and a return to a system like that could ease the lot of people are completely unrealistic.

3. Interview With Professor Julius Lipner

First Encounter

I think I first encountered the Hare Krishna movement in this country, in the UK. I was a student of King's College in the University of London, doing a PhD on the concept of the self in Indian and Western thought. I was doing this degree in the Department of the History and Philosophy of Religion, as it was then called, at King's. My wife and I came to this country in December 1971. It was all very new to us, and whilst we were trying to settle down, I had to plunge into my PhD work. We were living in South Kensington, London, and I had to travel to King's every week from there. During my journeys, or other visits to central London, I sometimes saw Hare Krishna devotees singing and dancing in the streets. I had come straight from India, so the concept of people in Indian dress singing the praises of God wasn't unfamiliar to me, as it must have been to the other Westerners who witnessed this. What was unfamiliar was that the singers and dancers were Westerners themselves. I kept wondering, "What are all these white folk up to, jumping around and singing in that way?" It was an entirely new phenomenon to me.

This took place at the end of 1971 and into 1972. That's when the movement first began to impress itself upon me. Then you read about it in the papers. Since I was interested in Hinduism, not least in connection with my PhD, I kept an eye on the movement, though I noticed that it tended to receive a rather negative and uncomprehending press at the time. Here were people acting strangely, away from their own traditions, and I wondered if this was a part of the hippie phenomenon, and if drugs and promiscuous sex had a part to play in it. I think I was swayed to some extent by what the press said or reported.

ISKCON has come a long way in 40 years from such misunderstood beginnings, and I've come a long way too in that period in my estimation of ISKCON. If I'm not mistaken, Bhagwan Rajneesh and his movement were also in the news then. People were not sure how to distinguish between the two. There seemed to be little doubt in my mind, from what I read and heard, that Rajneesh's followers were into permissive sex and drugs. But then ISKCON's own publicity, and a more tempered publicity about ISKCON in various written sources, got to work and slowly the realisation dawned that no intoxicants were allowed in ISKCON, and that strict rules about sex and marriage prevailed in the movement. And slowly the respectability of ISKCON as a religious way of life began to emerge, not in association with Rajneesh and his followers, but in contradistinction to them. Not only the reportage but also the images one saw about the two movements, one full of naked bodies in apparently drug-induced states, the other with devotees sober and clothed, were in sharp contrast.

I went through a learning experience from thinking of ISKCON as a problematic group to thinking of ISKCON as a movement that had credibility in its own right and that derived from the *sampradaya* of the Gaudiya Vaishnavas of Bengal,[1] that is, as serious, earnest people of faith. However, at that time I emphatically did not associate ISKCON with any form of scholarship, and I think rightly. I associated ISKCON, rather, with extrovert religiosity, a tendency to propaganda about their faith, and a largely Western following. But gradually ISKCON was setting itself apart from other movements associated with Hinduism in the West, many of which had the term "Tantra" attached to them, such as the followers of Rajneesh—though I realised later that even this was a mistake since genuine Tantra is hardly permissive but strictly controlled where ritual sex and so on is concerned. But though I didn't associate the Hare Krishnas with scholarship, I slowly began to look upon them with respect as a form of authentic Hinduism. However, I still didn't get a chance to study ISKCON properly.

That happened when I came to take up my lectureship in the University of Cambridge in 1975. I think I played some role in generating a perception of ISKCON as a respectable branch of Hinduism because I accepted an invitation to speak at an event in Inis Rath in Northern Ireland.[2] I was aware that by speaking publicly at this event I might be perceived as giving some legitimacy to this form of Hinduism, but I believed I knew enough about ISKCON to do this responsibly. I think it was Shaunaka

---

1   Gaudiya Vaishnavism (also known as Chaitanya Vaishnavism) is a tradition founded by Chaitanya Mahaprabhu (1486–1534) in Bengal, India. Gaudiya Vaishnavism concentrates on devotion (*bhakti*) to Radha and Krishna, and their many divine incarnations, which are viewed as the supreme forms of Deity (*svayam bhagavan*). Most popularly this worship takes the form of singing Radha-Krishna's holy names, such as "Hare," "Krishna" and "Rama," (most commonly in the form of the Hare Krishna mantra). As a branch of Gaudiya Vaishnavism, ISKCON's distinguishing feature is its chanting of the Hare Krishna mantra or *mahamantra*: Hare Krishna, Hare Krishna, Krishna Krishna, Hare Hare/ Hare Rama, Hare Rama, Rama Rama, Hare Hare.

2   This ISKCON temple community, which has a public retreat, is Govindadvipa Dhama on the island of Inis Rath in Lisnaskea, Derrylin, County Fermanagh, Northern Ireland.

Rishi Das who invited me. The experience itself at Inis Rath was a positive and instructive one—I went with my wife and still remember vividly the dancing by devotees in the temple there and the reverberating *kirtan*s sung outside after the temple ceremony; and I began to read and learn more. I later read the book edited by Steven Gelberg—*Hare Krishna, Hare Krishna*[3]—and became convinced that one was dealing with an authentic Hindu movement.

It occurred to me that the grief that ISKCON was still coming in for in some sections of the media was very similar to the criticism made against the early Christians, not to speak of such orders as the Dominicans and Franciscans in the early part of their histories. Certainly the behaviour of both traditions had striking parallels. Both lived an unusual lifestyle; both abandoned worldly forms of living; both dressed "strangely" in comparison to the general public; both followed strict rules about sex and food. And both initiated new forms of spirituality which, so far as the Christians are concerned, are now regarded as normal and even enriching. I said to myself, "These people, the ISKCONites, are doing the same thing. They are a fresh start in our societies from a Hindu point of view, and are going through the same birth pangs *mutatis mutandis* that early Christian movements went through." I now saw ISKCON with different eyes, and with increasing respect. You can't respect people you don't know.

I remember that some years after my Inis Rath experience, I was again invited by ISKCON to give a talk in Belgium at one of their centres. I believe it was an important talk for self-reflection in ISKCON because it was published in an ISKCON journal, I think; anyway I have seen it referred to in an ISKCON publication.[4] I remember seeing a number of teenagers from ISKCON families standing at the back and listening intently. And it occurred to me that I should say something that concerned them. So I spoke about the need for freedom of thought among the young in ISKCON, the problems teenagers face when they are not allowed to conform—perhaps for very good reasons—with their peers in the world, and similar issues, as well as how they might feel marginalised and neglected. I also spoke about the need for women in ISKCON to be shown respect in their own right, for them to be given a chance to take

---

3   Gelberg, S. J. (1983) (Ed.) *Hare Krishna Hare Krishna: Five Distinguished Scholars on the Krishna Movement in the West.* New York: Grove Press.

4   Lipner, J. (1994) ISKCON at the Crossroads? *ISKCON Communications Journal* 3: 22-4. Here Lipner suggests that ISKCON's future prospects are not very promising unless its members tackle two major problems, namely, (1) the status and role of women, and (2) the training of their children.

their rightful place as equals in the movement and to make a contribution on this footing. There were a number of senior *sannyasis* in the audience, but I carried on regardless.

I remember the kids crowding around me after my talk, agreeing with the points I had raised and saying that I had spoken what they were thinking, that they thought that their parents didn't understand their problems. The women didn't say much, but I hoped I had made them think. In fact, it was a woman devotee who later quoted from my talk in an article to support some of the points she was making. So that was good.

Changes, Developments and Future Prospects

All this is relevant regarding my memories of Tamal Krishna Goswami.[5] Tamal Krishna Goswami's affiliation to the Faculty of Divinity at Cambridge University did not come out of the blue. By the time he applied to do a PhD in the Faculty under my supervision, I had, as I have indicated already, acquired knowledge and respect for ISKCON as a religious organisation. But there were other factors involved in accepting him. One was Kenneth Cracknell.[6] Kenneth had become a good friend before he left for Brite Divinity School in Texas to become a professor there. He had connections with Southern Methodist University, also in Texas, where Goswami had done a BA in Religious Studies. Kenneth and one or two of Goswami's professors had spoken glowingly of Goswami's

---

5 Tamala Krishna Goswami (1946-2002), born Thomas G. Herzig in New York City, served on ISKCON's Governing Body Commission since its inception in 1970. In January 1972, he accepted the renounced order of life (*sannyasa*) in Jaipur. He served as GBC Secretary for India from 1970-74 and was appointed trustee of the Bhaktivedanta Book Trust, responsible for book sales in the USA. Tamal Krishna Goswami was also personal secretary to Bhaktivedanta Swami Prabhupada and authored several books on various religious subjects, including two classical Vedic dramas. Although he later became a doctoral student, focusing his thesis on the "Krishnology" of ISKCON's founder-*acharya* at the University of Cambridge under the tutelage of Professor Julius Lipner, he tragically died before completing his studies. In one issue of the *Journal of Vaishnava Studies* specifically dedicated to the life and work of Tamal Krishna Goswami, Professor Lipner, along with other scholars, has commented on his memories of Tamal Krishna Goswami: Lipner, J. (2003) The Pioneering Scholarship of Tamal Krishna Goswami, *Journal of Vaishnava Studies* 11 (2): 23-6.

6 Kenneth Cracknell, a Methodist minister, taught at Wesley House, the theological institution in Cambridge responsible for educating candidates in the Methodist ministry. He has also written about ISKCON, concentrating on practical points of interfaith work, as well as addressing difficulties faced by a missionary organisation like ISKCON in an interfaith setting: Cracknell, K. (1996) The Four Principles of Interfaith Dialogue and the Future of Religion, *ISKCON Communications Journal* 4 (1).

enthusiasm and academic ability, and this counted for much with me. Further, the fact that Goswami, a mature man of middle age, had taken the trouble to go through the mill, so to speak, and get a solid grounding methodologically and otherwise—for example, by acquiring Sanskrit—at the BA level in a good University also weighed with me. It occurred to me that in its five-hundred year history, the Divinity Faculty at Cambridge University had never had a student like Goswami—a Hindu monk—yet I thought that he should be given a chance. I knew that I was sticking my neck out, but I told Goswami that I would support him, and that if the Divinity Faculty's Degree Committee accepted my recommendation, I would act as his doctoral supervisor. He would have to continue to work on his Sanskrit, of course, but I would take him on. The Degree Committee accepted my recommendation, and Goswami was in.

Goswami's objective was to help start the scholarly ball rolling in ISKCON by getting a PhD from a top University, and I wanted to help him achieve this. He was a man of considerable influence in ISKCON, so he had a good chance of achieving his objective. I never regretted my decision. He was an excellent student—diligent, intelligent, and articulate. He wrote fine, precise prose, and fell into the scholarly mode with the minimum of fuss. He had all but completed his doctorate when he met his untimely death. But all was not lost. I spent quite a long time in the midst of my other duties editing his thesis for publication so that his work and ideas would not be wasted, and then handed it over to Graham Schweig,[7] his co-religionist in the United States, and a distinguished scholar in his own right, to round it off from within the field, and seek a publisher. I am delighted to say that the thesis will see publication before long, thanks to Graham's efforts.[8]

Goswami went down very well in the Faculty, and also in Clare Hall, a postgraduate College of Cambridge University, where I had helped him obtain admission. Not only in the Faculty but also in Clare Hall, he was the first of his kind, and he became a familiar figure in his saffron robes, and he made many friends with his genial manner among fellow students and the staff. He was a man of Jewish origin who had converted to

---

7   Graham M. Schweig is Professor of Philosophy and Religious Studies at Christopher Newport University. He was earlier Visiting Associate Professor of Sanskrit at the University of Virginia and received his doctorate in Comparative Religion from Harvard University.

8   Graham Schweig has recently overseen the publication of Tamal Krishna Goswami's previously unfinished Cambridge PhD thesis: Goswami, Tamal Krishna (2012) *A Living Theology of Krishna Bhakti: Essential Teachings of A. C. Bhaktivedanta Swami Prabhupada.* New York: Oxford University Press. Schweig himself has also included both a critical introduction and a conclusion within the pages of this important book.

ISKCON and become, as I have said, very influential in the organisation. He was Prabhupada's, the founder of ISKCON's, personal secretary, and the knowledge he acquired through this about Prabhupada's teachings stood him in good stead for his doctoral studies, which were on ISKCON's teachings and interpretations of Gaudiya Vaishnavism.

He told me that he was from the Bronx, and so had to be tough when growing up. I think it was this toughness under a friendly exterior that gave him the stamina and will to do his studies. What struck me was his willingness to take instruction from me, even though we were roughly of the same age. This deferral to his academic adviser also needed toughness to accomplish. For my part, I was determined that "this experiment" of taking on a Hindu *sannyasi* to study for the PhD in our Faculty for the first time should not fail. So between us we worked hard for a convergent end, and when his thesis is published I think you will be able to say that we succeeded.

Goswami was a pioneer. He told me once that he incurred misunderstanding and severe criticism from within ISKCON when he took up his academic studies and took time out to work for a PhD. I can understand that. A new religious movement takes time to build up an intellectual foundation with which it can properly challenge worldly values. The same thing has occurred in other, now more established religious traditions. This is why I called Goswami a pioneer, indeed a courageous pioneer.

The first phase is to consolidate the movement's spiritual life. I think ISKCON has achieved that, at least to an appreciable extent. But if the movement is to make a real contribution to this world, then it must deepen its spiritual foundation by intellectual reflection, which inevitably contains a measure of self-criticism. I mean this in the best sense. For such criticism is a purifying process, strengthening conviction and enabling one to learn from others. And this is a survival strategy, enabling the movement to propagate and grow. Goswami told me, "I want to serve my community by scholarship because that's the best way to understand it, and the best way others can grasp what it stands for. My faith can stand up to scrutiny, and I want to show that it can." Well, this suited me, for the method he proposed—objective scholarship, if you like, in a first-class environment—was the only way to go about achieving his goal.

It may have been no coincidence that the Oxford Centre for Hindus Studies—OCHS[9]—which is a respected academic institution with an ISKCONite foundation affiliated to Oxford University, and on

9   The Oxford Centre for Hindu Studies (OCHS) was founded in 1997 and is now a Recognised Independent Centre of Oxford University. Its main purpose is to develop academic programmes of scholarship, research and publishing in the field of Hindu

whose advisory committee I am pleased to sit, started up about the same time that Goswami registered to do a PhD. There may be no causal connection, but the point I am making is that both occurrences, the registration to do a doctorate by an influential *sannyasi*-member of ISKCON in Cambridge and the establishment of an academic ISKCON centre in Oxford, were symptomatic of a new phase in the development of the movement that was necessary if the movement was to thrive; it was pioneering at the same time. One begins to see genuine scholarship, much of it delving into the history and teachings of the movement, developing inside ISKCON or among its sympathisers around the world now, not only in the UK, but also in other parts of Europe, in the US, in India and elsewhere around the world. This is the only way forward.

There are disadvantages to this, of course. Such scrutiny is like a winnowing fan that upsets complacency and the mental laziness of some kinds of religious belief. Maturation is always a painful process. But its fruits are a deeper and more accommodating faith, and the ability to make a serious challenge to the materialist values of our modern societies. The trick is to maintain a proper balance between being part of the respected academic establishment on the one hand, and challenging the embedded materialist, consumerist and aggressive core values of so much modern living on the other. One must try not to lose this edge. The *Katha Upanishad* talks of the path of the good—as opposed to the pleasant—being as sharp as a razor's edge. A mature religious person has to learn to walk this edge.

If a religious movement, however, adopts the "drawbridge approach," seeking comfort in pulling up the drawbridge and turning its back on the world, it cannot function as a catalyst, as a lever, for change for the better.

Indian and Non-Indian Devotees

Indian Hindus in the diaspora crave an identity, both culturally and religiously. The fact that they are joining or sympathising with ISKCON in increasing numbers is to me a very positive sign. Forty odd years ago, when the movement was young and when I had come to the UK, there seemed to be no—or hardly any—Indian Hindus who had time for ISKCON. I think most of them had the same view as I had: suspicion and doubt as to what these dancing Westerners with Hindu robes and ceremonies were up to.

studies, although the Centre further aims to engage the Hindu community in the academic study of its own philosophy, education, and culture.

I made the point in my talk in Belgium discussed earlier that ISKCON should not hesitate to call itself a Hindu movement. I had heard that there was a debate in the movement about this, that some expressed a preference for being called "Gaudiya Vaishnavas" and not "Hindu." My point was that not many in the West had any idea as to what or who "Gaudiya Vaishnava" was, and that it was important, as the movement was maturing, to be located—in the West at least—under the aegis of a world religion such as Hinduism. Otherwise, they would have no voice. People have a voice as Christians, as Buddhists, as Muslims and so on; it was important, therefore, to have an identifiable voice as a Hindu. One could then distinguish further and say something like "A Hindu of the Gaudiya Vaishnava kind" or whatever; but one needed to locate oneself authentically within a world faith. In the world of inter-religious discourse, one needs a recognisable identity.

Today ISKCON is generally viewed as a respectable and authentic Hindu movement, and this is a mark of having come of age. Indian Hindus, especially in the diaspora, are very adaptable. They are prepared to give their allegiance or sympathy to a movement that they perceive as authentic, even if it is different from a tradition in which they were brought up, providing certain circumstances are right, and these circumstances include perceived authenticity and spiritual affinity. ISKCON should capitalise on this and see such allegiance as a mark of growing strength. And one way of adapting is to acknowledge that ISKCON is a "Hindu" movement in general, though a Gaudiya Vaishnava one in particular. This gives diasporic Hindus a voice as a recognised and respectable minority in the context of a majority community with different cultural and religious origins. This also gives ISKCON a better chance of survival and development in the interests not only of themselves but also of the whole community in which they find themselves.

Theological Challenges: Conservative and Liberal Perspectives

In considering opposing conservative and liberal approaches to doctrine and practice in ISKCON, I am tempted to say, "Look at the Anglican Church." The Anglican Church is riven by such controversies, as is the Catholic Church, though in the Catholic Church they are better at keeping such things under wraps. But such controversy is the mark of a mature tradition. If a movement is so small or regimented that it has only one point of view, it tends to die out. It tends to pull up the drawbridge of contact with the outside world, and it is eventually crowded out of existence. But if it is the case that the movement is growing and interacting with the world at large, it is bound to develop factions.

This, of course, can be both good and bad. A great deal depends on how difference is handled. I keep getting this unsolicited magazine called *Back to Prabhupada*. I find it objectionable because it is full of scurrilous and personal attacks on other ISKCONites, including on occasion, Goswami, who can no longer speak for himself. This is not the way to prove that you are right. Rather it is a shrill and immature way of making your point. Dispassionate argument is one thing, personal attacks are quite another. If you have a point to make, make it courteously, coherently and rationally. I've reached the stage of throwing this magazine directly in the bin now because I find it so negative. This is not the way to handle difference.

The right way is to discuss, debate and try and prove your point cogently. There may come a time when breaking point within a movement is reached. Sometimes that is inevitable. But it seems to me that even when this happens, the two factions should remain on speaking and dialogic terms, and this for at least two reasons, or perhaps three. One, outsiders tend to perceive both factions as part of the same tradition generally; so it does no good to resort to internecine warfare. The whole movement suffers adversely if that happens. Two, difference can be creative; so it pays to keep up the dialogue. It is misguided to think that difference is always divisive. And finally, it is doubtful if only one faction can be in possession of the whole picture or truth. One presumes that there are intelligent persons on both sides. So by remaining in conversation with good will, there is a better chance of a deeper, more complementary truth or understanding emerging.

In every mature community there will be conservative and liberal wings. One side is keen to preserve tradition and check untoward or headlong change; the other side tends towards making that tradition relevant to modern circumstances. *Virtus stat in medio*, as they say. A balance needs to be struck. That's what produces longevity in the end. This is why people like Goswami and institutions like OCHS are so beneficial to a growing tradition. They introduce the element of self-critical and therefore strengthening scrutiny to that tradition. This is only possible by applying scholarly standards, and following such researches, sometimes fearlessly, to their logical conclusion. If there's worth and truth in the subject-matter put under this scrutiny, it will then stand out and endure the test of time.

Women and Gender Roles

We live today in an age of globalisation. By this I mean simply that traditional barriers that were not particularly porous have now become porous. For example, the distinctions between international and national, national and regional, and regional and local have virtually broken down from the viewpoint of information technology. In the past, something that happened locally was reported locally. If it was important to spread that news, it took weeks if not months for that to happen. But today, a local event can become global in seconds through the Internet. Thus one's situation has the potential to change rapidly, and this must influence ways of thinking in organisations. Cultural and sociological changes become pressing, otherwise one runs the risk of stagnating and becoming irrelevant. And we can apply this to the role of women in ISKCON.

When I spoke at Inis Rath some years ago, I included comments about the role of women in ISKCON, as I mentioned earlier. I said that the women should be given the opportunity to play a full and creative part in the movement, that they should not be viewed as mere appendages to the men, or have only subsidiary roles. After all, they form about 50% of the movement, and it would be foolish to waste all this potential. And among the women present at that talk, at least, I believe that my comments were well received; for, as I said earlier, my encouragement to them was reported in an ISKCON publication written by a woman.

The argument may be made that Prabhupada himself was conservative in his estimate of what an ISKCON woman should be permitted to do. Perhaps, but Prabhupada spoke nearly half a century ago. Whether you believe that he was the *sadguru*, that is, the embodiment of divinity in our midst, or not, is not quite the point. The point is that he spoke to be effective in his times. If he was too revolutionary, he wouldn't have been listened to, and then his message would not be effective at all. So what he said all those years ago must be investigated to see if it harbours the seed for innovative and realistic change with the passage of time, and scholars of ISKCON must be prepared to scrutinise his words to see if this seed of change for the role of women in ISKCON is present, and if it is, enable this seed to be nurtured so that its growth can be made relevant for current times. This is how movements adapt and survive, and this kind of mature reflection is part of the critical investigation of true scholarship I was talking about, and on which people like Tamal Krishna Goswami had embarked.

I see this issue—that is, the role of women in ISKCON—as having parallels with the issue of the role of women in the Christian churches, with particular reference to the question of whether they can be ordained as priests. Some argue that the twelve apostles chosen by Christ were all males, therefore only men can be ordained priests. But this argument lacks depth and misses the point. Further, it does an injustice, I think, to Christ's teaching. Christ was constrained to function, however innovatively he may have done so, within the realistic possibilities of his time, otherwise his teaching would not have been effective in the prevailing social contexts. Further, his teaching was based on the premise, notwithstanding the social circumstances of his time, that all humans are equally the image of God, which presumably means that irrespective of gender they have the same spiritual privileges and rights. But such rights are not abstract entitlements—they must be translated into social practice, and this would include, today at least, the right for women to function as priests and so play their rightful and necessary part in the evangelisation of the world.

I believe that women should be encouraged to play a full role in ISKCON's life, academically, socially and in every other way. Anything less would be to stereotype women in a denigrating way. I would be surprised if this went against the spirit of Prabhupada's teaching.

Concluding Thoughts and Reflections

Organisation is indispensable. If a movement is to survive and grow, it must have a certain level of organisation and institutionalisation. For this provides the ability to control growth and give a sense of internal and perceived identity. Someone once said, "If all things are possible, then nothing that happens will be interesting." So there must be a measure of control of belief and practice. Then we will have interesting results. This is what the concept of "tradition" is about. Further, organisation will enable proper self-criticism and the processing of such reflection. This is what ISKCON is now struggling to achieve, and, as I see it, with a good measure of success. It has acquired an important voice for good in this world, and its members require self-control to prevent disintegration and squabbling.

4. Interview with Professor Kim Knott

First Encounter

When I was doing my PhD on Hindus in Leeds,[1] initially I conceived of that as being a study about Gujarati and Punjabi Hindus, mostly focused around the Hindu temple in Leeds, but then working outwards into the community. But I felt, after a while, that this wouldn't be a full account of Hinduism in the city, and I was really interested in exploring and researching all aspects of Hinduism. So I decided to look at any new initiatives. And the Hare Krishna movement didn't have a substantial presence here, but some of the other movements did: Transcendental Meditation, for example, and the Brahma Kumaris, who at that stage were going under the name of Raja Yoga. They were very active in Leeds; so I did quite a lot of participant observation with them. But I also looked at groups that had a smaller presence, such as the Divine Light Mission, which had quite a few events organised back in the late 1970s and early 1980s. The Hare Krishna movement used to make forays into Leeds, particularly from Scotland; so they would tend to appear here on a Saturday and do their missionary work in the city centre. But that seemed to me nevertheless worth reflecting upon. I, therefore, included them very briefly in my PhD work.

When I finished my PhD, Peter Clarke at that point was developing a series on new religious movements with Thorsons, and the branch was called Aquarian Press at the time. He asked me if I would write a book on the Hare Krishna movement. Although I didn't know much about it, nobody who has just completed a PhD and gets commissioned to write a book would say, "No," blithely. So I thought, "Although I don't know much about them, why not?" I had been down to Bhaktivedanta Manor and had met devotees up here. And I thought it was a nice challenge and a nice offer to be commissioned to do this. That's where it started, resulting in *My Sweet Lord*.[2] It was a book I really enjoyed writing. It was my first book. I had published my PhD, but that was very much written as a thesis;

---

1   Knott, K. (1982) *Hinduism in Leeds: A Study of Religious Practice in the Indian Hindu Community and in Hindu Related Groups*, PhD Thesis, University of Leeds.

2   Knott, K. (1986) *My Sweet Lord: The Hare Krishna Movement*. Wellingborough: Aquarian Press.

so *My Sweet Lord* was the first book I wrote. It was my first piece of participant observation and interviewing and fieldwork beyond my thesis.

My first dealings with the movement revealed a proselytising instinct. I was quite struck by that. So when I agreed to do the book I expected to be proselytised to, and there was very much that feeling in relation to the Hare Krishna movement. There was an anti-cult response to the Hare Krishna movement at that time. So there was very much a view that, when you meet them, they're going to sell you books; they're going to want to make you into a devotee. That was very much the spirit at the time, both in the media and in the anti-cult response to the Hare Krishna movement.

Interestingly, my first encounter was with a group of Indian Hindus. That's obviously a really significant development since that time—the engagement of Indian Hindus in Britain and the States and elsewhere. But my very first encounter was in a pilgrimage party of Hindus from Leeds down to Bhaktivedanta Manor; so I was encountering the movement from that perspective right from the very beginning.

Changes, Developments and Future Prospects

The link with Indian Hindus has developed very significantly. Another change has been that shift in focus away from aggressive, outreach-style activity. There is still that outward presence but less around very overt fundraising to a softer *sankirtan* approach.

I saw the whole zonal *acharya* system at its peak,[3] and obviously that's changed very dramatically and no doubt in many ways for the better in terms of the health of the movement. But it has to be said that it was a very exciting time and accompanied by a lot of cultural activities; a lot of festivity; a lot of unity around the idea of the guru; a lot of affection and emotional engagement in Leeds, particularly with Gurudev[4] and his entourage. One side of that is the attractiveness of it all, even at the same

---

3   The zonal *acharya* system was the dominant form of leadership in ISKCON from the time of Prabhupada's demise in 1977 until the mid-1980s. It was an autocratic system, with different gurus having authority over ISKCON centres in separate zones or regions or the world. After a series of problems, the zonal *acharya* system was reformed in 1987 and greater authority was thereafter invested in ISKCON's Governing Body Commission.

4   Gurudev, better known as Bhagavan Goswami, joined ISKCON in or around 1970 and became an ISKCON zonal acharya. In the 1980s when Kim Knott was doing her research on ISKCON the "zone" for which he was responsible included a number of regions, namely, Britain, Belgium, France, Spain, Holland, Greece, Italy, South Africa and, finally, because of his origin, Detroit in America.

time that it leads to all sorts of potential problems: individuals finding difficulty in their own pursuit of the principles of the faith, and so on.

One of the things I was interested in doing, even in *My Sweet Lord*, was reflecting on the new-not-so-new idea of the Hare Krishna movement. And I think that's still very pertinent, but it is less necessary to do it these days. Back in the early 1980s it was very important to make people aware that this wasn't just a new movement, with no links to the past, and with no theological engagement with an earlier history in the Hindu religious tradition. So I think one of the stabilising aspects in looking at the Hare Krishna movement has been that engagement with studying the wider *bhakti* movement within Hindu studies: the Chaitanya movement, Gaudiya Vaishnavism, and so on. That's still very important for understanding the Hare Krishna movement. If scholars are going to make a contribution, that's not to be forgotten.

But the other important aspect about understanding the Hare Krishna movement, which is something I have made a contribution to, alongside the contributions of lots of other scholars, is in thinking about the Hare Krishna movement as a modern movement. Srila Prabhupada capitalised on modern technology, the possibility of global movements and some of the processes of globalisation. The Hare Krishna movement is what it is partly because of its ability to make use of those processes. They are important for understanding the movement.

Today "fond regard" is, I would say, the public perception of the Hare Krishna movement. I'm not in it, but I would say that's what it feels like from an insider's perspective. The public quite like to see members of the Hare Krishna movement out on the streets, thinking that they're part of our social history, that they're part of that history from the 1960s onwards, particularly in London, but even in the other cities of the UK. Recently, for example, a piece of public perception that I heard about was from someone who was at the Wave Demonstration[5] in London the other day and who said, "Thank goodness for the Hare Krishna movement; they were out there feeding the flock in Trafalgar Square."

So people today do have a kind of fond regard. And there certainly isn't that public fear that there was back in the first half of the 1980s about the Hare Krishna movement. But, of course, there are some problems with that, too, as a public perception. The movement can become a part of cultural heritage; and from a theological point of view or from an impact point of view, it might become quaint and part of the archive, whilst

---

5 The Wave Demonstration in London took place on 5th December 2009. Demonstrators who took part in the event called upon the British Government to take action on climate change.

not necessarily being seen to engage with the things that matter. There's always a double-sided possibility here. Cultural heritage, I think, is one of the ways in which a secular society deals with religion. It makes religion part of the cultural heritage. That's a good thing because it domesticates it and makes it comfortable for people, but at the same time it can disempower it.

Ways in which ISKCON is now written about and researched and seen publicly mean that I don't think you'd ever get the same kind of media anxiety and moral panic around the movement that you might have got before. Then again, you *might* if something happened. We've seen this in the States, for example. You've only got to have a negative event. We've seen this in the Catholic Church with cases of child abuse, and you have that in the Hare Krishna movement and elsewhere in other traditions. So something like that happens and you are straight back on page one of the newspapers again. There is a new stability around the public perception of ISKCON, but, as with any religious organisation, that could change very quickly. Any religious organisation is expected to uphold certain levels of moral practice, and if they fall down from that then they could find themselves on the front page. And that's just a permanent issue for all religious organisations.

If we were trying to think of the Hare Krishna movement in the narrower sense of it—not so much its wider lay audience but a more specific group of individuals who become initiated and want to live in a temple—then the future might be quite challenging. It's difficult for me to say, but it is around those issues of transmission that stand out. It used to be mostly about mission and proselytising but obviously now it has to be more about nurturing children within the movement and those kinds of issues. And also one has to think about the relationship between the committed few and the much wider lay public. So I don't expect to see it disappear from the scene, but it's about being flexible and open to change.

ISKCON has definitely played a role in terms of interfaith involvement. I remember articles from *The Irish Times* and so on about Shaunaka Rishi Das' work in relation to interfaith activities of one kind or another.[6] It has been exemplary and hugely important. If you also think of the role of someone like Akhandadhi Das on BBC Radio 4's *Thought for the Day*

---

6   Shaunaka Rishi Das in 2004 played the lead role in interfaith work that resulted in the publication of ISKCON's Interfaith Commission document, entitled *ISKCON and Interfaith: ISKCON in Relation to People of Faith in God*. Oxford: ISKCON Communications. ISKCON's five-point interfaith statement, together with remarks about ISKCON's mission, its theological approach to dialogue, and its principles, guidelines and purposes, are all outlined in this publication.

and so on, particular devotees have placed themselves in very important positions in respect of speaking Hinduism to a wider public. Not just in relation to interfaith dialogue but in relation to school education there is, in addition, the work of Rasamandala Das.[7] And in the case of a wider body of people who want to hear from Sikhs and Hindus and Muslims in that kind of public context, people who can articulate those religions are needed. There have been some key ISKCON people in those kinds of roles. I have admired the way that the Hare Krishna movement has been involved in that kind of interfaith work and how it has taken an interest in participating in debates about religious education.

Of course, a cynical person would look at any group involved in those kinds of activities and think about what is in it for them. There are always reasons why movements or individuals get involved in various interfaith projects, because it's important to being well-placed politically in order to represent the interests of that group going forward. So it's been both admirable and canny to have done that. I'm not for one minute trying to suggest that these are not genuine interests that the Hare Krishna movement has. I know these people very well and so I know the interests that they have are genuine.

One point that comes out of this, about these kinds of figures—and this would be true for any religious organisation—is the importance of key players. All religious organisations, just like all political organisations, can often be focused around key people who become symbolic and iconic in certain areas of activity. And that is what we are taking about here. Obviously, a challenge for a movement is then to find figures to replace them as they get tired or retire. ISKCON is as good as its key players in these fields; and finding their replacements will be important for ISKCON's future.

Indian and Non-Indian Devotees

The presence of Indian Hindus in the movement is something that's been there from the beginning, from the foundation and with Srila Prabhupada himself. In the UK Indian patronage has been there right from the very

---

7   Rasamandala Das (Ross Andrew) has some seventeen years' experience in education and teacher training and is co-ordinator of ISKCON Educational Services. On matters of education he has authored both articles and created resources for use in schools. Key examples of his work include the following: Das, Rasamandala (1998) *Towards Principle and Values: An Analysis of Educational Philosophy and Practice within ISKCON, ISKCON Communications Journal* 5 (2); and Das, Rasamandala (2002) *The Heart of Hinduism: A Comparative Guide for Teachers and Professionals.* Aldenham: ISKCON Educational Services.

start. That's been a central part of the development; that symbiotic relationship has been very important with the Indian Hindu community in
Britain. If you look at the provision of services and festivals and *pujaris* and so on within the movement, you see it's very important. But, of
course, from the point of view of that foundation in the States—when
Srila Prabhupada identified with a group of young people who were willing to listen to him and willing to take a risk in following him—that's the
other side of the movement's history. And, in a way, it would be very sad
to see that go. All the while you still have people who have been in the
movement for 40 years, 30 years, 20 years, and so on. Those voices and
that history and those understandings still represented there suggest the
question: How would the movement go about appealing to a new constituency of people like that? Also, what could be the relevance of the kind
of way of life that the Hare Krishna movement can offer to a new group
of white or young non-Hindu people? I think it's quite difficult to answer
here because in the early days, part of what was on offer was not just a way
of life but a community to live in. I suppose it will depend upon whether
those same notions of community appeal to people today and whether
they are on offer in the way that they were back then.

It's very difficult, as I have indicated, to separate the future prospects
of ISKCON from issues about who the Hare Krishna movement actually
appeals to these days. But the future of the movement is inevitably bound
up with its Indian base. Those people from Indian heritage communities who feel that the Hare Krishna movement represents the Vaishnava
tradition they're attached to will obviously be drawn in. Even if they're
not themselves Bengali, nevertheless they worship Krishna or some other
aspect of Vishnu; and the Hare Krishna movement fits into their frame of
reference. So in terms of that broader constituency, I can't see any problem for the movement going forward as long as it retains its willingness
to work with that broader constituency and to represent the interests, to
some extent, of that broader group.

It should equally be noted that Indian Hindu communities in the West
are themselves changing. It's not the same as it might have been 20 years
ago, and the new Indian Hindu heritage people coming to the movement
are themselves different from their parents' generation. That in itself will
mean a change. And maybe it's not exactly more of the same—more of the
"old" same, as it were—but neither does it mean the Hare Krishna movement is becoming a kind of established sect of Hinduism that doesn't
represent a new shift. That in itself probably represents a new direction.

Also, the new generation of *gurukulis* and the Pandava Sena were very important at the time of the campaign for the Watford temple[8] and so on. It was a major interface between a wider non-Hindu, non-ISKCON public and the movement itself. This was about opportunities—providing, ensuring and securing opportunities for young Hindus. They have been a vital part of the Hare Krishna movement politically in this country. That's probably a group for ISKCON to target in terms of the development of the movement and going forward. Because the Indian Hindu community in the UK is not the same now as it would have been 20 years ago, the second and third generations are hugely important, and they have very clear ideas about the way they want things to go that may well be different from their parents. They are key to ISKCON's success in the future.

Theological Challenges: Conservative and Liberal Perspectives

From a scholarly point of view, debate regarding liberal and conservative ideas in ISKCON is of great interest. From the perspective of a scholarly observer, those engagements, exchanges and battles are fascinating. They make the substance of work for a scholar. In terms of the people I've known within the movement and who I've probably worked with more than others, they tend to be on the liberal side, both here and also in the US. But I have learned a lot from some very strict devotees in the past, devotees who have probably gone on to be thorns in the side of ISKCON to some extent. I've learned a lot about religious life in general from those people and why they make decisions to be rigorous, conservative and perhaps more traditionalist in their approach. It's been illuminating to be around those kinds of people and challenging because those are the ones who usually immediately say, "And what about you?" That is, they can be very personally challenging.

I think some of these conservative/liberal issues ISKCON has had to face and deal with, it will continue to have to face and deal with. There's no doubt about that. I know that just from some of the posts that continue to come through my mailbox. It continues to focus on issues of guru

---

8   For one whole decade (from 1986 to 1996) Bhaktivedanta Manor near Watford fought a long but successful campaign against Hertsmere Borough Council. Hertsmere Borough Council endeavoured to prevent Bhaktivedanta Manor from being a public place of worship. The Manor's successful campaign received an endorsement in 1996 from John Gummer MP (the Secretary of State for the Environment at the time), an endorsement for plans to build an access road, enabling worshippers to continue to use the ISKCON temple.

reform and the movement in its schismatic branches and so on. That is often where you get some of these conservative/liberal issues emerging. But, speaking as a scholar, I would have to say that, unless a movement can be flexible and accommodating to change, it isn't going to survive, except for a very small handful of people. That's not to say that traditional aspects of religions are not very comforting and very attractive to people. We can see in quite a number of religions—maybe the more traditional aspects of Catholicism or Anglo-Catholic aspects of the Church of England—that there's always a niche there that's very important for some people for whom the radical end of change isn't what they feel comfortable with. So there's always an extent to which a group has to continue to supply and make space for those kinds of people who have this sort of need, and who want and relish the more traditional aspects. But at the same time, if a movement can't change, it won't go forward in the future. So it's hard to say whether one or the other really is correct. I've always admired "Cleaning House and Cleaning Hearts," the article by Ravindra Svarupa Dasa[9]—that idea that ISKCON has to clean itself up and embrace change at the same time.

If you remember the language of articles like "Cleaning House and Cleaning Hearts" it was very much to try to differentiate between innovation and a willingness to accommodate yourself to change. Have there really been theological or philosophical shifts in ISKCON? It was not so much about giving up your key principles and practices but finding a means to engage them in a new way within a wider society or the demands of a new generation of people. There have been lots of practical attempts to engage with change, but a lot of the principles seem to me to have stayed the same and to have stayed at the heart of ISKCON.

The key thing—and you get this in all religions—is the process of interpretation, whether it's in Judaism or Christianity or in ISKCON. There's a freedom to interpret what is core, but it's a freedom within certain guidelines. It is the extent to which a movement feels secure in and of itself to enable people to interpret and maybe doubt openly, and not be clamped down upon or not be stamped out or thrown out at the first sign of some questioning. That's the sign of a sophisticated, more secure movement.

I remember going along to ISKCON Communications conferences in Belgium, where the issue of people feeling that they needed to have a space to be able to raise doubts was really aired. That's hugely important for any

9   Ravindra Svarupa Das (1994) Cleaning House and Cleaning Hearts: Reform and Renewal in ISKCON. *ISKCON Communications Journal*, two part essay, 3: 43-52 and 4:25-33.

religious movement. If you want people to stay with you, and you can't hear their doubts and their questions, then don't expect them to remain because they'll go and express those doubts and questions somewhere else. It's absolutely part of the natural development of any individual to ask those kinds of questions in terms of spiritual journey.

Schismatic challenges are just inevitable. The history of religion shows us that all religions have had to face schisms, and they do it in different ways. So the Catholic Church has been masterful by-and-large at coping with, embodying and carrying forward schisms within its wider body and within its wider community, by only expelling individuals. Of course, there is always the risk that if you expel an individual a group will grow up around that person. We know that from the Gaudiya Vaishnava tradition more broadly. So there is within Gaudiya Vaishnavism—indeed within the whole Vedanta tradition of Hinduism, where you get schismatic moves—certain charismatic figures who can lead a group forward and so on. It's an inevitable part of the theological tradition that ISKCON is within.

It's just a question of how ISKCON then decides to treat schisms and how rigidly it draws its own boundary. Obviously, if a movement draws a very rigid boundary, then it may force people out. Maybe the consensus is that it's important to do that, but maybe the consensus sees that it is important to have a slightly fuzzy boundary so that you can keep more people in. Possibly drawing out rigid boundaries would be viewed as the right thing to do, to preserve the identity and the heritage of the movement. That is something the movement itself would have to decide in relation to whatever the issue was.

Women and Gender Roles

I think in the Hare Krishna movement now there is less of a focus on the issue of gender than there was in the past. Maybe that's partly because debates about feminism have changed. Feminism isn't quite on the agenda in the way that it was. So it doesn't appear as a social criticism of ISKCON in the way that it might have done, say, in the 1980s and early 1990s. Of course, there were always women in the movement who occupied very important roles and who were widely respected; and I get the sense these days that there is plenty of scope for women in ISKCON.

Yet they still have to deal with a teaching about gender in the movement which is certainly open to very conservative interpretation. But then I think there have been plenty of people who have argued against that kind of more conservative interpretation. There's plenty of evidence, not only from those phrases of Prabhupada that are often trotted out, where he might have expressed something that on the face of it might have seemed negative towards women; there are plenty of examples, too, where quite clearly he didn't actually hold that view in practice. There have been sufficient debates about this subject now for ISKCON to be fairly confident—and for women in ISKCON in fact to be assured—that they could reach their fulfilment within ISKCON.

But, of course, having said that, you could find a temple or a group of people who might still be trotting out some very traditionalist line, which might be detrimental to women achieving their potential. There is always that possibility within all religious movements. There is less focus on it now, both for external and internal reasons. I don't think that there is anything intrinsically within ISKCON that would suggest that women couldn't have a full active and very rewarding life there. But obviously that will depend on their actual practical situation, where they are based and all the rest of it.

There are some key players who certainly made the case by their lives and actions: some of the early women in the movement, for example, and their recollections of Prabhupada show this. Once women started to mobilise and organise within ISKCON, particularly in the United States, that certainly helped because it enabled them to get together to voice their concerns, to develop an agenda, which they could then take and engage the GBC in. Some of the points where women actually became involved as temple presidents or adopted important teaching roles, and taught classes, matter.

There have been lots of little steps along the way. The Women's Ministry, which came about 10 years ago, is important. But, as I say, the much more day-to-day activities of supervising individuals who are taking class for the first time, and taking up important administrative positions, really showed that women could do those jobs. And when they had the respect of their male colleagues and their support—all that would have helped as well. Still, a lot of the names that you think of in relation to ISKCON are men. So we'll see in the future whether women get more of these positions and whether they become some of the key figures.

If you think about what has happened in the last 20 years in Christianity in the UK—just in the Church of England, let's say—where women have been able to be ordained and have central roles at parish level and quite a lot of administrative roles as well, it's completely changed the face of Anglicanism within Britain. For many people, Anglicanism is about what those women deliver locally. Their key mentor is a woman. ISKCON has got a long way to go before it really achieves that, but I see no reason why it shouldn't or couldn't. It will be up to the individuals within ISKCON to bring it about. There has been a lot of controversy in the Anglican Church, of course, but the controversy hasn't stopped that grassroots change from happening. That's been because of considered decisions within Anglicanism. But it's equally kept that space open for those individuals who didn't want that to happen. So it's kept the "flying bishops" who would not ordain women. And now we see the Catholic Church saying it's going to open a space—or wants to open up a space—for disillusioned Anglicans. But the face of Anglicanism has been massively changed by women moving into those roles. Who knows whether that's had any impact on the slide in numbers or anything like that? But certainly for many practising Anglicans, the face of their church is a female face now. The feminisation of Anglicanism has gone a long way in the last 20 years.

All this will definitely feed into debates about Hare Krishna. The external world will continue to ask questions about this. Even though it may not be feminists or sociologists of religion who are saying ISKCON is not a place for women to be, for example—because there certainly have been some of them—there will be other people with whom devotees engage asking those questions about gender. It will keep the movement on its toes. If it wants to have that outward engaged way of working, whether it's around education or interfaith relations or whatever it might be, it's inevitable.

It also opens the door to other questions, like the question about homosexuality. Of course that's a very important one. There's always going to be the next issue emerging on which any religious organisation is going to be asked to face and address it, and it has to find out what its view is. It probably will have a mix of views. The debates obviously change. Sometimes I get to the point where I think, "What could happen next? What could the big issue be next?" We have had all those debates around sexuality and about gender. What could be the next thing on the agenda that religions have to deal with? You never can tell until that actually happens.

Concluding Thoughts and Reflections

The issues of transmission and mission for ISKCON, or for any movement thinking ahead, are crucial concerns. It is very much about getting the message out and the question of who it wants to go on getting its message out to. These issues about change and mission are obviously central for any movement to face. If one thinks about the Hare Krishna movement in the past from a proselytising focus, to one in which ISKCON later developed a congregational face and began to engage more with the Indian Hindu community, then the issue of how it begins to think about how it nurtures its own young people—its own children within the move-ment—is important. Can it hold on to its own children? Does it want to? And what does it do to achieve this? How many of those young people will stay? So there are the issues of transmission and nurture as well as mission; and what should be emphasised is whether there is still some-thing the Hare Krishna movement has to offer to people who have yet to discover it. Important considerations here are whether there are new ways to do that or whether the old ways are still the best ones—relying on the strategy of *sankirtan* and so on.

I particularly want to put children and transmission on the agenda. How they will change is important. I have often thought about the young people in the Krishna Consciousness movement in terms of how they will possibly grow up and think of themselves as Hare Krishna devo-tees—maybe even think of themselves as Hindus. Let's say some of these people go away and go to university, and they think of themselves as mem-bers of the Hare Krishna movement, and their parents articulate that, but they are not anywhere near any big Hare Krishna centre. How are they going to sustain that commitment and identity at a distance? Of course, that raises the issue of online community and virtual community.[10] There is a group of people who meet on a regular basis here in Leeds. But to what extent will they take recourse to other Hindu organisations, for example?

The Unitarian Church, for example, depends a lot on its electronic net-works. I think some of the smaller religious bodies inevitably do. There are quite strong traditions of them having learned to operate in a networked way with whatever technological resources are available. It's hugely impor-tant. A woman whom I met in ISKCON left the movement, and one of the things that touched me was how important Bhaktivedanta Manor was to her and how tragic she felt it was to have to leave it. Bhaktivedanta Manor was her sense of place. And if you believe in the deity who manifests locally within a given temple—if you believe in Radha-Londonishvara[11] or whatever deity it is, the deity who manifests and who has that local liv-ing presence—you need access to it. That's why that electronic presence can be very, very important for people at a distance who feel that they can access their deity in that way. Whatever you decide about this practice

---

10 Today many major ISKCON temples and festivals can be streamed live and viewed on the internet. For example, see www.mayapur.tv.

11 Radha-Londonishvara are marble images of Radha and Krishna installed in 1969 by Prabhupada in Britain's first ISKCON temple at Bury Place, Bloomsbury. The deities have since been reinstalled and are now at London's Soho Street temple.

you can get some engagement with the representation which is dear to you, even if it's not the full experience that you're getting by accessing it online. I think it will be very important for people who feel attached to particular divine forms, particular *murtis*. Online *puja* is huge and will be crucial in shaping spirituality and religious identity for young people growing up in ISKCON now and in the future.

5. Interview with Dr Kenneth R. Valpey

First Encounter

I first saw devotees chanting Hare Krishna on the streets of Berkeley, California in the late 1960s. I had minimal interaction with them but I was at the time—as were many other college students—dabbling in Indian philosophy, yoga, and so on. I was reading a translation of the *Yoga Sutras* by Patanjali with a commentary from the Theosophical Society. And whoever it was who wrote this commentary mentioned *bhakti-yoga* several times. That stuck in my mind. I was wondering, "What is this *bhakti-yoga*?" Then, in the summer of 1972 in Germany, I had started travelling. I had quit school. I was working over in Germany, wondering, "What next?" And I thought, "I wonder if those Hare Krishnas are here somewhere? Let me see if they are. If they are going to be in Germany, they are likely to be in Heidelberg." So I went to Heidelberg, and I saw two devotees on the street in the town square chanting Hare Krishna. I asked them, "What is this all about?" And they said, "We practice *bhakti-yoga*." Immediately, I thought, "I think this is what I have been looking for." I joined the next day.

After some days the devotees got the news that Srila Prabhupada was coming to Paris. All the German devotees were going to meet him there. By this time I was also wearing a *dhoti*, or loincloth, and had a shaven head. It was just natural that I would go along. On the way, I was asked, "Would you like to be initiated?" I couldn't think of any really good reason why not. This was three weeks into my devotional career. And I said, "Yes." Then, when I met Prabhupada, I felt confirmed that this was the person I was looking for. He was on a higher level of understanding of life; and I thought that I should surrender to him. So I was initiated at that time.

Changes, Developments and Future Prospects

There is one key change that has occurred in ISKCON. I'm not entirely convinced that it was a good change, and it was as follows. When I first joined the Hare Krishna movement, we would go out wearing *dhoti*s. We would do *kirtan*—group chanting—up and down the street and then we would stop for maybe half an hour and we would distribute Hare Krishna magazines. And then after half an hour or so we would again go up and down the street with our *mridangas*—drums—and *kartals*—hand-cymbals—and we would sing, going back and forth. That changed.

At some point, certain devotees got more and more involved in distributing books, and then came the idea that you could distribute them better if you didn't look like a Hare Krishna; and that meant no *kirtan*, as well as no Hare Krishna clothes. I personally always went along with whatever was being done and said. That was my mood: really to try and surrender. And we got word that Prabhupada approved of this. But ever since that change, I've felt that maybe something was gained but also that something was lost.

Another major change over the years, which Rasamandala Das has written about, and which is in the book edited by Dwyer and Cole,[1] is the demographic change: devotees migrated from the temples and changed the colour of their *dhotis* from saffron to white.[2]

But I think yet another important change that has come about in more recent years—and it's related to the last point—is permeability of boundaries, and that's happened for many reasons. The Internet is certainly one reason; and another is a move towards religion or spirituality that involves picking and choosing what you like. Whereas in the beginning a person would come and join the temple—and that meant becoming isolated from the outside world—now that's just not possible. The *bhaktas* or devotees just go on to the Internet and check out what everybody is saying. So that's a significant change.

The first time, for example, that I was confronted or struck by the presence of media in relation to deity worship was not so long ago: at the end of 2001. I was just finishing my doctoral research in Vrindavan. An ISKCON swami came and invited me to go with him to Jaipur. We stayed at one quite well-to-do businessman's house, and they had on the television a broadcast of the *arati* of Radha-Govinda, the main Krishna temple in Jaipur; and it really struck me that you could watch the *arati* from television. Also, somebody made a funny little clip about that sort of thing on ITV. It was about getting up in the morning and, instead of going to

---

1   Andrew, R. (Rasamandala Das) (2007) (Comment On) Moving into Phase Three: An Analysis of ISKCON Membership in the UK, in G. Dwyer and R. J. Cole (Eds.) *The Hare Krishna Movement: Forty Years of Chant and Change*. London and New York: IB Tauris, pp. 54-67.

2   The expression "devotees…changed the colour of their *dhotis* from saffron to white" refers to the shift in ISKCON membership or affiliation from ascetic devotee to householder devotee, a shift which started in the early 1980s and which is even more pronounced today.

mangala arati, it showed someone just turning on the TV and lying in bed playing *kartals*. But I wouldn't negatively judge it. I think there is a sense that Krishna can work through any media.

Speaking of people in their homes, of course, the other phenomenon is that now in ISKCON every home is a temple; everyone has their deities and is doing *puja* at home. That's going on. In one article that Tamal Krishna Goswami wrote[3] he points out that, with this shift of locus of spiritual life from the temple to one's home, there is also a shift of spiritual authority. But in that shift there is an opportunity to perhaps cultivate one's own spirituality in a deeper way than would be possible in a more regimented temple situation.

In Germany in the early years, we were viewed as a kind of pious terrorist organisation. We were having what we called "blitz *sankirtan*." We would have 11 devotees in one van, and we would pull up in a village, park the vehicle, pile out and do what I have just described: going up and down the street, doing *harinam* and distributing books. And within an hour we'd be all back in the vehicle again and driving to the next village. But when the long arm of the law caught up with us, that ended. We were not doing legitimate business, misrepresenting our activities. We were doing what we were told by our leaders. We were saying we were collecting for poor people in Bangladesh. So that all caught up with us; that became a huge court case in 1975, but most of the charges were dropped.

Then we got attacked through the newspapers for months and even for years. It seemed that they never stopped. It seemed as if they had nothing else to talk about. And one of the ideas that came out of the newspapers was the sense of panic, the idea that there must be thousands of these Hare Krishnas. That's what they perceived in Germany at the time, and this is perhaps with good reason because we would go into a village as explained and do what I have just stated and then we would simply disappear. But we were not more than about 60 or 70 devotees in the whole country at the time. So perceptions are interesting.

Perceptions have changed now, certainly. I haven't been keeping up with how it's all going in Germany but I know a lot of things have been done to repair our reputation. There's the whole work of ISKCON Communications, for example. My feeling is that here in Britain, at least in the London area, one can walk around in devotional clothes and people won't look twice. I think now we are seen as innocuous, pious, slightly goofy, but well-meaning and part of the landscape of weirdness. We're

---

3   Goswami, Tamal Krishna (1997) The Perils of Succession: Heresies of Authority and Continuity in the Hare Krishna Movement, *ISKCON Communications Journal* 5 (1): 10-27.

seen as being on the good side. That said, of course, in England with the strong Hindu factor, I think that we are also quite well respected.

But it also has to be said that for the vast majority of people, we in ISKCON are inconsequential. I noticed this when I first went back to school in 1995 at the University of California-Santa Barbara. It just struck me one day that the vast majority of people in the world have never even heard of Hare Krishna. To me it was a revelation, having been in this little bubble of ISKCON for so many years, to then step out into a large public university. It struck me that there's a huge gap between perceptions within this little Society of ISKCON and perceptions outside it. Hare Krishnas are often now publicly viewed as wacky, well-meaning but harmless.

I'm not sure I like the terminology of words like "holding on to" when thinking about ISKCON membership. I think it could be self-defeating if ISKCON members feel "We need to hold on to our people." If, on the other hand, the feeling is, "Let us serve, let us nurture, and let us be helpful to our people," then that's much more positive. If ISKCON feels it needs to "hold on to people," as it were, then that's going to be the beginning of not holding on to them. When people feel, "I'm being held on to," then the first thing that they do is start making arrangements to be let go of.

One important thought expressed to me just two weeks ago was by one of my godbrothers, one of my mentors for deity worship. He had relatively recently visited an ISKCON temple in Germany, where he had being doing deity worship many years before and for many years of his devotional life. I asked him, "What is your impression of the deity worship now?" He then said, "What struck me was that the temple was empty." And his point was that *pujaris* are not acting or functioning as *via media*[4] to the congregation. Therefore, the congregation doesn't come forward. The priests are not ministering to the congregation, not counselling them, not acting as *brahmanas* to them.

---

4   The term *via media* (or in its full expression *transparent via media*) is typically used in the sayings and writings of Prabhupada to denote the role and status of gurus or spiritual masters. (See, for instance, Prabhupada, A. C. Bhaktivedanta Swami (1977) *The Science of Self-Realization*. London, New York, Los Angeles, Bombay: Bhaktivedanta Book Trust.) Here Prabhupada writes: "For example, I can see the letters of this book...through these transparent eye glasses, without which I cannot see because my eyes are defective. Similarly, our senses are all defective...(W)e cannot do anything without the via medium of the spiritual master. Just as a defective eye cannot see without the via medium of spectacles, so one cannot approach the Supreme Lord without the transparent via medium of the spiritual master." (ibid. p. 283). Kenneth Valpey appears to extend use of the term *via media* to apply also to the work of priests, one of whose tasks it is to bring devotees into contact with Krishna in a temple ritual context, the role of priests in the ritual setting thus mirroring the work of gurus in the domain of teaching.

One additional issue I have noticed speaking from the *pujari* perspective—and I was Minister of Deity Worship for some time in ISKCON—is that the status of the *pujari* in ISKCON is that of pious custodian, and not much more. It seems to me that this could be changed and would be something that needs more attention for a longer-term expansion of ISKCON if we are thinking in terms of having a focus on temples. Why do people go to a temple? Why not just have deities in the home? The temple in a sense is just a big headache to maintain. It's expensive. It's so much trouble. Why, as devotees, do we not just have our private temples? There has to be a good reason for public shrines.

In our ISKCON tradition the centre of the temple is the deity. And who is serving the deity most closely? It's the *pujari*. If a *pujari* is not trained to be a *brahmana* in the broader sense of connecting people to the deity so that they feel someone cares about them, and therefore that the deity cares about them, then this is a huge problem. We see in many parts of the Western world that we have empty temples for most of the week. There is, of course, the busy Sunday programme but then, once again, it's empty for the week ahead after that. It seems to be that could be changed but requires a shift in understanding and, in my view, with emphasis on education.

Part of that shift is the reason why I turned from deity worship to education. I felt that to be an important key—if not *the* key—for ISKCON's continuation, expansion and for setting roots in wider culture. What is important is that it develops its own education programmes. So Bhaktivedanta College Radhadesh in Belgium[5] is a small step, but it will eventually start showing some effects. Right now some people question, saying, "What's the use of this?" But I think that it will lead to something significant. And we also have in India the Mayapur Academy[6] training *pujari*, which is equally important.

---

5   Bhaktivedanta College is located in Ardennes, a rural region of Belgium. The College was opened by ISKCON in 2002 and in the future hopes to become a Vaishnava university. The main focus at Bhaktivedanta College is the study of Vaishnavism, and it has a strong ministerial programme, which trains and educates devotees to become preachers, teachers, leaders and managers. It also currently offers a BA Honours course in Theology and Religious Studies and will soon make provision for BA Honours courses in Educational Studies and in Business Administration.

6   The Mayapur Academy at ISKCON's world headquarters in West Bengal is an educational institution and was established in accordance with the express wish of Prabhupada specifically to provide training in deity worship and in the performance of *samskaras*, as well as offering training in *brahmanical* culture, cooking, arts and sciences (www.mayapuracademy.org).

On to another point—ISKCON has an interfaith statement that has been officially accepted by the GBC. But it seems to me that there are different levels of interfaith interaction. My own doctoral supervisor at the Oxford Centre for Hindu Studies was Francis Clooney, and he has become quite a prominent figure in theorising about comparative theology. I have been influenced in a positive way by some of his ideas. One of his ideas—I think a basic idea—is that, if you really want to do anything comparative, interfaith work or whatever, you have to allow yourself really to be affected by the other. If you think you are going into interfaith to sell your religious message, it's not true dialogue. One of the things we have at Bhaktivedanta College is a course on interfaith; so this might be going in the right direction. We also have lots of qualified people in this country like Kripamoya Dasa, who has done a lot in that area.

But ISKCON here has mainly played a role with the attitude that, "We are going to show everybody what matters," a very missionary kind of role. I think one way this could be changed over time is if devotees individually and collectively could think more deeply about the question, "What is it that we have to offer to society?" This matters instead of one prominent idea that a lot of devotees have expressed, namely, that ISKCON is some kind of hegemonic institution that's got everything. It is a problem to assume that those from other religions have got to come into it in order to get what ISKCON possesses; and if they don't, they are then somehow seen to get nothing spiritually meaningful. This stance is changing, but it needs more articulation. It needs to be more explicitly expressed that we can be participants in a greater society. The first step is to recognise that there are good, sincere, intelligent people in the world who are not chanting "Hare Krishna" and who are not ever going to chant "Hare Krishna." But they can hopefully appreciate ideas that devotees have. They can perhaps even adopt certain aspects of those ideas, consciously or unconsciously; and, like that, the International Society for Krishna Consciousness can become more influential as the lessons are learned of avoiding an all-or-nothing programme of missionary zeal.

Indian and Non-Indian Devotees

The increasing presence of Indian Hindus in ISKCON should be an impetus for non-Indian leaders to become more familiar with Indian culture, and that means learning Gujarati, for example, and spending more time in India amongst the kind of people who are in their congregation in order to get more of an understanding of how their culture works. This also means reading more about Indian history and politics and philosophy so that they can really relate.

I have just been in Hong Kong. We have a really interesting situation there. There are some 30, 000 Indians in Hong Kong. The ISKCON temple in Hong Kong is small, and it has a Chinese Hong Kong congregation and Indian members. On Sunday we have two programmes there. One is at mid-day, mainly geared for the Chinese; and one is in the evening, mainly geared for the Indians. So all members have been accommodated in that way. They then have two kinds of shifts in the same temple.

At Bhaktivedanta Manor in Britain, for example, it has been my impression that some of the older non-Indian devotees have felt sidelined because of the attention that is given to the Indians. This, I think, is to be expected. The attention to the Indians is understandable, and the feelings of those who are not Indians are equally understandable. Maybe more effort to do something to bring the non-Indians back in is necessary. But it is natural that people create their own congregations. I think if non-Indians become less involved it would be a great loss. It would be unfortunate because it would mean Prabhupada's intention was sidelined. Prabhupada definitely wanted that his movement would not be just for Indians.

If ISKCON decides to focus on the Indians, then it's going to be Gaudiya *maths* who will take up the Westerners. But right now the majority of leaders, the gurus, and so on are non-Indians. And one thing I've noticed is that the different places I go in the ISKCON world reveal that you get different congregations depending on which gurus are present or visit. Maybe *that* is how it's going to be. It's not something that you can try to control or regulate. But how to safeguard particular groups I'm not sure about. If Westerners see that it's only Indian gurus in ISKCON most of them will not be attracted to them. Yet, as indicated, most leaders and gurus are still non-Indians. So it's also about empowered preaching and teaching. At Chowpatty in Mumbai, for example, people go there because of the teaching that goes on, especially the preaching of American guru Radhanath Swami.

Theological Challenges: Conservative and Liberal Perspectives

On matters of liberals versus conservatives in ISKCON, I would say that it's important that there is the cultivation of an atmosphere where things can be openly discussed. Again, that gets back to the point that there has to be education; there have to be forums where ideas can be discussed by people who have thought deeply and not simply superficially about these matters. There is always something to be said positively about a conservative argument; and there is similarly something to be said about a liberal argument—or something in between. For me, the question is always, "What is behind the questions when investigating debates about conservatives and liberals?" What's not actually being said here is actually the key.

One of the projects that we have been developing is called ISKCON Studies Institute. We have a conference once a year. We have a journal. It used to be known as *ISKCON Communications Journal*; now it's called *ISKCON Studies Journal*. It's just in its beginning stages. It's hard to get it going. It's difficult to get people writing articles, and so on. But the idea is to have a forum that is not under ISKCON control of any kind. There's no GBC funding or anything of that nature. It's a kind of an independent think tank. But it's ISKCON friendly; it's for helping ISKCON. It's for academic devotees to feel free to think and talk. We have a formal annual conference on a certain topic, and it's open for anyone to come and listen. But the selection of speakers is done just like in an academic conference. Presenters are given a certain amount of time to speak and a certain amount of time for discussion. I think there needs to be more of that so that we can all learn to speak more clearly. Devotees tend to oversimplify an issue: it's thus with many devotees either-or; it's this way or it's not, and so on. With a lot of these debates—conservatives versus liberals—to me they're about undigested material, and what are really needed are some better tonics for digestion.

As to the matter of the ISKCON Revival Movement and splinter groups, I think it is part of a bigger dynamic and that is the marketplace of faith. You have different shades of understanding, and then those mainly become more pronounced under different pressures. Then you've got a group for whom one idea is especially important, or one particular person is important. My only concern with all of this is that ISKCON keeps its boundaries. It's natural for any society to have boundaries. But they should be relatively permeable. The more ISKCON tries to build up walls to separate, it becomes self-defeating. You suddenly notice that you are surrounded by a big wall and all you want to do is get out. Even though you are told how safe you are or how whatever it is that is said is to ensure protection, it becomes self-defeating.

I'm a member of a GBC committee and it's called Vaishnava Community Relations Committee. For all of us on this committee, it's very important that avenues of communication be kept open for interfaith dialogue and intrafaith dialogue as well, helping everyone to see that whatever differences we might have, theological or otherwise, people who have a faith are all sincere souls. They have their perspectives, and they should be respected somehow.

Women and Gender Roles

Take the role of women. I think we should question ourselves. Why do we have that expression, "the role of women"? We use it very much more in relation to women than we do in relation to men. We don't hear about the role of men very much. We talk about the role of women. Why is that? We should try to see what is behind such questions.

Nonetheless, I have women disciples, some of whom I have heard quite a bit about in terms of how they have suffered in temple situations. I have women disciples who have done service for years in temples and then pretty much been left on their own, and I am speaking of women disciples of my own here in the UK. For many years I have thought that it's a mistake and irresponsible for temples to take unmarried women in as temple residents in an unlimited time frame. It seems to me—and this might also apply to men, but I see it especially with women—that sometimes they'll be attracted because they don't have a clear picture of their future. They'll just be persuaded with the words, "Just surrender to Krishna." So they'll come to the temple, and they'll be taken care of reasonably well in the temple for a certain amount of time but, as a result, they become disempowered. They can thus no longer take care of themselves.

I think this is a huge mistake. Then, suddenly, they become a liability to themselves. At some point they don't belong in the temple. They should be married, but for one reason or another, they don't want whoever is on offer for marriage purposes, or whoever is out there doesn't want them. But it suddenly becomes a temple problem, which it shouldn't have been. It seems to me that they should come to the temple as an educational institution. They should get training for a one-year period or for a two-year period. After that the devotee should get some form of recognition and told, "We wish you all the best in your spiritual life," and also told, "We may counsel you about how you might go on from there." This might mean advice to go back to school, to get married—this, that, different options. Especially for women this message is important but also for men it stands.

I think all this is being done gradually. I've heard, for example, in Hungary that they have a farm programme, and there is a whole series of steps before someone can become fully a member of that farm community.[7] And even then, after four years it's understood that it's time for residents to go. Only if someone really persuades the community that they really want to stay on can they do that.

This is not a new idea. Prabhupada spoke in the 1940s in the *Back to Godhead* magazine of temples being places of education. He wanted temples to be the places where people got training. But because we in ISKCON have got this dynamic of wanting to increase numbers, and also becoming economically dependent on their service, then we lose track of the actual interest of the devotee.

But regarding the position of women in ISKCON, I think changes have clearly taken place. There has been much more of an understanding that women are not simply *maya*.[8] There has even recently been a GBC resolution, saying a woman can be a guru. But I spoke to one senior woman who would be a likely candidate. I asked her, "Are you going to be a guru now, *mataji?*" She said, "No way." "Why not?" I asked her. She then said that she wouldn't want to do it because there's too much negative attitude in the greater society against it. She wouldn't want to have to battle with that, and she also said that this same feeling is found amongst her god-sisters who might be considered for that role. So no woman wants to be a target for that kind of negative reaction. But that could change over time. I could well imagine that perhaps there's one woman who thinks, "I don't care what they say," and maybe she will have many respectable disciples, too. In that case, then, but maybe also later, it is possible.

Concluding Thoughts and Reflections

Years ago one ISKCON swami suggested an interesting model of ISKCON which I found very helpful to think about things generally. That is, ISKCON has three dimensions. There is a kind of ground floor, which is everything, we could say, that is physical and visible about ISKCON, including the organisational aspects. There is the next floor, which is individual *sadhana* or the cultivation of spiritual life that devotees undertake and with which they feel some satisfaction. And then there is a third level, which, we could say, is most invisible. That is the level of Chaitanya Mahaprabhu's spreading of the *sankirtan* movement all over the universe

---

7   The biggest ISKCON centre in Hungary is its rural farm community. This is located in Somogyvamos, a small village in south-west Hungary.

8   The term *maya* (meaning "illusion" in Sanskrit) has sometimes in the past been used by male devotees, especially brahmacharis or sannyasis (monks), to refer to women and also to refer to the material world. The term's derogatory employment was, therefore, always denigrating to women.

in the sense that something is going on beyond anyone's control. It's a spiritual movement, and no matter what we do or don't do, think or don't think, it's going to go on. And it will go on in ways that we may never be able to imagine or expect.

One thing I've seen is that devotes get overly concerned about that ground level, and instead of Krishna Consciousness, the focus becomes ISKCON Consciousness. But there needs to be more attention to the second level, and that is manifesting itself. One way it is doing this is that we see different retreats that have happened. We see Sacinandana Swami,[9] for example, having his *japa* retreats. We have summer camps in Eastern Europe where so many people come and hear devotees giving seminars and going in-depth with different *tapas* or austerities. We also have many conventions and the like. But more energy could go into that. There's a lot of energy put into the mechanical side of things. If the movement is going to attract people, *as* a spiritual movement, then there has to be a sense that it's really spiritual in terms of personal practice, personal experience, true realisation, and so on.

At the last ISKCON Studies Institute conference the theme was the guru. And at the conference there was some discussion about guru in relation to *shastra* (scripture), a technical discussion. So, why do we need ISKCON? Why do we need an organisation? Why do we need an institution? We don't really need it at all. Strictly speaking the guru-disciple relationship doesn't need any organisation. It can do without it. But why do we have ISKCON? My theory is that Prabhupada wanted there to be a Society that would foster the development of *sadhus*. *Sadhus* are non-political; they only care about cultivating spiritual life and in bringing spiritual life to others. That's what would be attractive to people and that's what will make the Hare Krishna movement influential and respectable. So that's my message. My point is that the issues that come up around guru, for instance, will all naturally find their place if the emphasis were a bit more upon *sadhu*, or the culture of a *sadhu*. I think that's what the greater society needs more than anything. The greater society doesn't want gurus as such; they want *sadhus*. They want people who are simple, renounced and wise and who are not thinking in sectarian ways. For ISKCON to have a successful future this message is key.

---

9   Sacinandana Swami is an ISKCON *sannyasi* guru of German origin who joined ISKCON in 1970 and who was initiated by the movement's founder-*acharya*. He is a celebrated ISKCON teacher and writer and has translated the *Bhagavad Gita* into German.

6. Interview with Steven J. Rosen

First Encounter

Growing up in Brooklyn, New York, in the 1960s, I was more or less a normal kid. That is to say, I had all the usual interests and involvements that most other kids had, from playing with friends, board games, comic books, music, and the like, to a warm family life, with a good home, loving parents, and caring siblings. But I always wanted to know what life was really all about. That might be what distinguished me from my peers early on. I had this gnawing desire to understand why I was here, and whether life was defined by some overarching purpose.

From the time I was about eight or nine years old I started asking the questions, "What is life all about? Why do people act the way that they do? Why do they think the way that they do? Is there a God? Why am I here?" All those kinds of questions plagued me—not to the point where I wouldn't do what normal kids did, but the questions were always lingering in the background, and I needed to know the answers. So I started reading books and looking into the various religions of the world.

By the time I was a teenager I was quite well-read, and I was looking for the source of religious truth. I had an inherent distrust of organised religion. When I looked at Christianity, to take one example of the many religions, I saw that it began at a certain time in history—2000 years ago—and that there was a founder—Jesus. In other words, the world's religions began at a certain point in time, and their scriptures were compiled at a particular date. And this is true for all the different religious traditions. But what intrigued me when I encountered Hinduism, or the religions of India, is that here was a religious tradition that couldn't be traced to one particular founder at a particular point in time, and I thought, "This seems to be what I am looking for—a universal, non-sectarian spiritual tradition that doesn't have a historical dimension like the other religions do." This was all prior to meeting the devotees of Krishna.

The idea of *sanatana dharma* really intrigued me: the eternal function of the soul. I wasn't interested in sectarian religious beliefs. I was interested in who we really are and what life is really all about. I then met Krishna devotees when I was in tenth grade and on my way to high school—the High School of Art and Design. I met Madhusudana, a very

93

early disciple of Prabhupada, though I didn't know this at that time. I was sitting on a train reading an edition of the *Bhagavad Gita*—not Prabhupada's but another edition—and Madhusudhana walked up to me and said, "That's poison!" I immediately looked at him like he was nuts. I then said, "You are into Eastern philosophy, aren't you?" I knew enough about the Hare Krishnas to recognise that they were interested in Eastern thought and that their tradition came from the East. So I asked, "Why poison?" And he said, "*Bhagavad Gita* is as pure as milk but even milk when touched by the lips of a serpent becomes poisonous." I thought then that he was obviously making a statement about the translator and commentator of the particular edition I was reading. So I asked, "Do you have a better edition?" And he pulled out Prabhupada's huge *Bhagavad Gita As It Is*. I said, "You are clearly going to try to sell me that big *Gita*, but I don't have any money." I was just a high school student after all. He replied, "I will give it to you as a gift; but all I ask in exchange is that you read it and then on Sunday come to our centre and let me know what you think of it."

I did as he said, and I was impressed. The Introduction to Prabhupada's *Gita* alone clarified so much. I had read a number of editions of the *Bhagavad Gita*, and I had no idea who Krishna was, no idea who Arjuna was, no idea what the battle of Kurukshetra was. But on just reading Prabhupada's introduction to the *Gita* all of that became clear to me. I saw it as something special, with information not available anywhere else. In addition, Prabhupada was articulating the *sanatana dharma,* or the eternal function of the soul that I had been looking for in all the different religious traditions.

I did go to the temple the following Sunday, and, while I had a good experience overall, I was left with many questions about the devotees. I thought that it was too fanatical, too extreme; it was not something that I wanted to get involved in. But the devotee who gave me the book was very smart. Madhusudana said, "I can see that you're unimpressed with Krishna Consciousness, with the movement. Come back next week. Our teacher will be here. Just do it for me." I liked him, as he seemed to be a very sincere soul. So I agreed to come back one more time the following week. When I came back Prabhupada was there and he gave a lecture. I felt something move deep within me. I thought, "This is my eternal spiritual master." After the lecture Prabhupada then came out of the room—I was standing in the hallway—and he turned and looked straight into my eyes and said, "Hare Krishna." I felt something touch my soul.

Prior to that, I was a sceptic. I had met different gurus from India and different religious leaders but nothing touched me like that. So that is the sum and substance of the story of how I became involved. Then I spent some two years coming to the temple, moving into the temple and moving out of the temple. This was a very volatile time in my life. It was the early 1970s. I was not even 20 years old, and so I was also interested in pursuing material life, as a young man is wont to do. Making a commitment to Krishna Consciousness was very difficult for me at that point. Yet I saw truth there, and that kept me engaged in Krishna Consciousness.

The Hare Krishna movement being young when I joined it—the movement was founded in 1966 and I joined it in 1972—was like many young religious movements: somewhat extreme, zealous and fanatical. But I never bought into that. When I joined the movement there were many devotees who had an "us" and "them" mentality. Just before I joined the movement I read Mahatma Gandhi's autobiography, *My Experiment with Truth*, and I felt that that was what I was doing in the Krishna Consciousness movement. It was frustrating with the devotees around me because once you joined you were expected to tow the party line. You would hear, "Krishna IS God" and "Prabhupada IS a pure devotee," with emphasis on the word "IS" and the verb "to be." You had to make these claims, and I just couldn't do that. If a devotee would say, "Krishna is God," I would say, "Yes, maybe." It was never a definite foregone conclusion for me. I was making an experiment. And because the experiment was very profound, because Prabhupada *is* a pure devotee, and because Krishna *is*, in fact, God, all that stuck with me. The experiment was not over and I feel that in many ways I'm still experimenting with truth. But now it is 38 years later, and I have had internal experiences—gone through a spiritual evolution—enabling me to see more of the truth of Krishna Consciousness. It took many years. I was certainly not like the devotees around me who were saying, "This IS the truth," back when I first joined.

Changes, Developments and Future Prospects

How the Krishna Consciousness movement has changed is profound. As with my own experience, it has matured. It grew and expanded. I don't mean numerically; that is not what I am talking about. It grew and expanded in terms of maturity, with its adherents coming to see that Krishna Consciousness is really a pluralistic, or at least an inclusivist religious tradition that acknowledges all spiritual seekers and all truths whatever the label or sectarian designation. A Christian mystic is also Krishna conscious; a Jewish mystic is Krishna conscious; a Sufi is Krishna conscious. These are labels for the same thing, and they basically refer to developing love for God on a very deep level. That can be expressed in various languages according to various traditions, but it is all Krishna Consciousness. That is acknowledged more nowadays.

Today the movement is recognising more its own inherent philosophy of universalism and non-sectarianism. In the old days devotees would say that they were non-sectarian, but they really had an "us" and "them" mentality. Now they have come to realise the very deep statements of the scriptures and the teachings of Bhaktivinoda Thakura and Srila Prabhupada, that truth is really non-sectarian; and it can manifest itself whether you are part of ISKCON or part of other religious traditions.

The movement today is a facility for people even of other religious traditions who want to further themselves in the science of God consciousness. What I have in mind when I say this—and this is a very tangible example—concerns the yoga communities throughout the West. In these communities there is an emphasis on *kirtan* or chanting the holy name. There are popular *kirtan* singers like Jai Uttal and Krishna Das[1] who have popularised *kirtan* in the modern world. And ISKCON is now seen as a place where these *kirtan* people can go, or where the yoga people can go. Here in New York we have regular 12-hour *kirtan*s once a month. Twenty years ago if there was a 12-hour *kirtan* in a Hare Krishna temple it would have been attended only by Hare Krishna devotees. Now the 12-hour *kirtan* is attended by people from yoga centres and from all different types of religious communities. The movement has here realised its own philosophy in broadening its welcoming mat to all groups of people. That is a very important development regarding the Hare Krishna movement today.

But public perception is a very complicated phenomenon because it depends on how educated a given individual is. I would say that, by and large, the movement did not become as popular as it had hoped to become. So in terms of public perception, most people hardly know what it is now. Most people have some vague recollection of the Hare Krishnas going out selling books at airports or seeing them as some sort of weird cult. These are uninformed people. But for people who are informed, like the people in the yoga community, they have come to see the Hare Krishna movement as the authoritative inheritors of a very specific yoga tradition—*bhakti-yoga*.

---

1   In America, Jai Uttal, a musician and singer-songwriter, and Krishna Das, a vocalist, have both been influential in popularising Indian devotional music and the performance of *kirtans* as well as *bhajans*. They have been and continue to be especially popular today in yoga centres in New York and also further afield in the US.

Now, of course, religious scholars also understand the Hare Krishna movement as the legitimate representation of a branch of Hinduism or of Vaishnavism. When I joined the movement scholars had no clear idea of what the movement was. They thought that it was simply a new religious movement. In the West this is true, but it is ages old in India and going by the name of Gaudiya Vaishnavism. So with modern perception I would say that those people who are informed about the Hare Krishna movement have a very good perception of it, seeing it not only as a legitimate form of Gaudiya Vaishnavism but also as a standard mode of Eastern spirituality.

In the early days recruiting followers was cultish. I mean, as mentioned already, you were either "in" or you were "out." You were either a monk living in the temple or at best you were a *grihastha* (householder), but a very monk-like *grihastha* living near the temple and taking part in temple festivities every day; or you were a *karmie* in *maya*[2] who had no connection to Krishna Consciousness. But because the movement has matured and has come to realise its own philosophy, by and large recruitment is defined a lot differently now. It now emphasises whether someone appreciates Krishna Consciousness and whether someone understands its value. If you do, you are counted amongst the followers.

This is very interesting because Lord Chaitanya Himself says in the *Caitanya-bhagavata* that anyone who even appreciates the chanting of the holy name is to be counted amongst the devotees.[3] So it is not that one has to be a regular chanter, wear robes or shave the head. No. If you simply appreciate the chanting of "Hare Krishna" or even if you like it, you are then to be counted amongst the devotees. It seems that is what the movement has internalised at this point in time. Of course there are some old, stodgy fuddy-duddies who cling to the internal ISKCON perceptions of the past and who will still think like that—that you are either a monk or you are "out"—but those who take this position are now few. The new generation of devotees and the visionary devotees of the past—the larger ISKCON these days—have a much broader perception about what it means to recruit, and it hinges on this appreciation factor to which I have referred.

---

2   The term *karmie* employed to refer to non-devotees, and the term *maya* used to denote the material world outside the Krishna Consciousness community, were commonly heard in ISKCON centres during the 1970s, denoting values of total opposition to society beyond the temple doors.

3   *Sri Caitanya-bhagavata* is a chronicle of the life of Chaitanya Mahaprabhu (1486-1533) written by Sri Vrindavana Dasa Thakura and translated into English by Sarvabhavana Dasa, Vrindavan: Rasbihari Lal, 2001.

Not everyone is inclined to live as a monk; so people can simply become a "friend" of Lord Krishna. We used to have the concept of FOLK—Friends of Lord Krishna, an acronym for a subdivision of this idea. I know people who now take initiation into Krishna Consciousness simply on that basis. They work a regular job; they have families; they live in the world; they can't get to the temple much. But because they deeply appreciate what Krishna Consciousness is, there are gurus in ISKCON who will initiate them, asking them to try to chant a certain number of rounds and to try to build up to sixteen and to follow the full principles.[4] It is nowhere near as strict as it used to be. Some followers might criticise this as a compromise, but it all depends on what kind of spin you put on it. You could call it "compromise" but you could also call it "accommodation." There are many words that could put a positive or a negative spin on it. But it really is simply acknowledging that people *are* people, that people *are* different. Not everyone is going to approach Krishna Consciousness in the same way, and that is fine. The philosophy gives enough leeway that people can be who they are and still progress in Krishna Consciousness.

What initially attracted me about Gaudiya Vaishnavism and ISKCON—and what continues to attract me still—is that it also includes a detailed science of how to approach God. I don't use that word "science" loosely. It's a methodology, a procedure, and progress can be gauged in the developing of one's consciousness in a particular way. It's very much a scientific process, and you don't find that in other religious traditions, at least not to this degree. I am talking not just about the writings of Prabhupada but also of his predecessors like Bhaktivinoda Thakura and Vishvanath Chakravarti Thakura.[5] Then, of course, there are the *Puranas* and the earlier texts like the *Mahabharata* and the *Ramayana*. In these literatures and in the people who fostered them you find a detailed science of love of God.

What role will this play in inter-religious activity? And what effects will it have on people from other religious traditions? I see a time when people will come to Krishna conscious devotees as professors of religion,

---

4   These principles include not eating meat, fish or eggs; not gambling; not taking intoxicants (including alcohol, tobacco and even tea and coffee); not engaging in illicit sex (meaning sex outside marriage or even sex within marriage if not performed for purposes of procreation). In addition to these four standard regulative principles, an initiated devotee is also expected to chant at least sixteen rounds of the Hare Krishna *mahamantra* daily on *japa mala* beads given to a devotee by his or her initiating guru. This means chanting the mantra a minimum of 1,728 times every day.

5   Vishvanath Chakravarti Thakura (1626-1708) was a Bengali Gaudiya Vaishnava leader who authored a number of devotional books as well as produced studies of poetry, rhetoric and grammar.

real professors who know how religion works and how to gauge genuine spiritual advancement. I see this happening already, albeit on a very small scale. I mentioned before the different yoga communities who come to the ISKCON temples to chant. Interestingly, they have also come to ISKCON devotees—myself included—to learn the science of *bhakti-yoga*. This is an amazing breakthrough, that people from Eastern communities, like the yoga groups referred to already, are coming forward. But I think Western religious communities too will come to appreciate the idea that Gaudiya Vaishnavism is a very detailed science of love of God, and they'll start to come and accept devotees as authorities on the subject; and they'll learn deeper aspects of their own traditions through Krishna Consciousness.

A true pluralistic tradition—and I do believe that Krishna Consciousness is truly a pluralistic tradition—will benefit here. It's part of the quality of humility not to think that you have everything but to recognise that you can benefit from others. Take the principle of *bhakti* or devotion, for instance. *Bhakti* is found in all religious traditions. So if a Christian cleric comes to an ISKCON temple to learn something about *bhakti* that cleric will also teach something about *bhakti*. This is because it is infused in all different religious traditions. Years ago, I myself was Minister of Inter-Religious Affairs for Brooklyn ISKCON, and this meant that I would go regularly to meet with rabbis, priests and imams, and they were always ready to learn from me about the Vedic tradition. But I always walked away with something from them too. I learned much from them about spirituality and what it means to open your heart to God. Individuals learn these lessons in their own ways. So whoever you interact with, you can get something from them and learn how to incorporate it into your own spiritual life.

Moving on to the subject of ISKCON youth, I see something very positive here as well. I feel that they have learned from the mistakes of the devotees of my generation. They are less fanatical by and large. There are, of course, exceptions, but I am talking in general. They are ready to accommodate others. They are not extreme. They tend to embrace Krishna Consciousness with great practicality. That is very valuable. It will sustain the movement in the future. Fanaticism could have destroyed the Krishna Consciousness movement in the past and at times it came very close to this. But even the fanaticism and the various problems that came close to destroying the movement in the big picture can be seen actually to have helped it. It may have humbled some devotees—and ISKCON's self-perception became humbled too—but, in short, I believe that the new generation of devotees and the youth that surrounds ISKCON are going to flourish because of their practicality and because of their ability to learn from the mistakes of their predecessors.

Indian and Non-Indian Devotees

Regarding the increasing involvement of Indian Hindus in ISKCON I have mixed feelings. On the one hand, it is inevitable because Krishna Consciousness is a legitimate part of the Gaudiya Vaishnava tradition and Indians living in the West especially are going to see it as their home. It's something that they are familiar with. In the West it's still an alien thing to many people but in India it is well-recognised. Hare Krishna devotees, Gaudiya Vaishnava monks, and those who are associated with Gaudiya Vaishnavism—this is all quite common for Indians; so it's inevitable that Indian Hindus living abroad would find and embrace it. That's good. This development also added certain legitimacy to the Krishna Consciousness movement because people see that all these Indians are recognising it as part of their own tradition, originating from India itself. That's equally very good.

But on the negative side—and this is something that upsets me, and I know it upsets many devotees from the early days—it almost seems counter-productive in our trying to show that Krishna Consciousness is non-sectarian and universal. It's not Hinduism. So there are a lot of "Hindus" taking part in Krishna Consciousness activities who seem to foster the misconception that Krishna Consciousness is some kind of Hindu sectarian tradition. It's not meant to be that. It's meant to be the science of love of God. That idea was clearer in one sense when I was a young devotee because few Indians were involved in it. When one encountered Krishna Consciousness at that earlier time, the newcomer may have believed it was some strange "cult" or, alternatively, they may have seen it as some kind of deep spirituality that only committed people were involved in. In a way, the Hindu involvement today contradicts those two points of view. It fosters the misconception that it is merely "Hindu," or another sectarian religion. Of course, it is not a new cult, either. It is deep spirituality, pure and simple.

Hindus have helped ISKCON financially and in many other ways, too, lending it, as I have indicated, a certain sense of legitimacy. This has helped ISKCON to be seen not as some new cult but as an ancient religious tradition, and Indians themselves recognise that.

Theological Challenges: Conservative and Liberal Perspectives

I think that both liberal and conservative approaches are important and that the movement has been sustained by having adherents who embody both. You need your liberals and you need your conservatives. They help each other, in fact, and they balance each other out, and they make the movement vital and healthy. I myself am hopelessly liberal, and I am using that expression with full awareness. We have to be open and liberal and understand that Krishna Consciousness is a person-to-person phenomenon. It has to be applied to all devotees individually. You can't make a pat answer or a pat approach for everything, and liberality is called for. But that being said, if we are too liberal, then we could lose the essence of what Krishna Consciousness is trying to teach.

This also relates to the prior points about the youth. While my overall thought is that they are practical, the danger, of course, is that if you are too practical or too liberal, you can lose the essence; and so I worry about the youth in their practicality, worry that they might override certain principles that help one sustain one's Krishna Consciousness. I will give an example of what I have observed. I see that a lot of the youth love *kirtan*. They are more involved in *kirtan* than many people from my generation ever were. But they are not so fond of chanting *japa*, the sixteen rounds, or of following the regulative principles. They may do it out of commitment, but my fear is that they may embrace those aspects of Krishna Consciousness that are pleasurable—after all who doesn't enjoy singing and dancing?—and they may reject the austerities. This is the danger.

I welcome the conservative faction of the movement and those devotees who promote this because they'll keep other devotees in line. As for me, if I see a young devotee who likes *kirtan* but who is not inclined to follow the four regulative principles, my thought is to let them enjoy what they enjoy, and if they insist on breaking the principles, well, then so be it. As long as there is some aspect of Krishna Consciousness that they like, they can make advancement. That's me as a liberal. But a conservative who sees them loving the chanting but breaking other principles will take them to task for it. They are not going to say that it's acceptable. This may discourage the newcomer altogether. Therefore, I say we should fan whatever spark is already there. The rest will come in due course.

Importantly, the philosophy of Krishna Consciousness *is* what it is. It's always been the same. There might be changes in approach, but Prabhupada was very clear what the philosophy was from the beginning;

so the philosophy has not changed in any kind of fundamental way. That is one of the things I like about Krishna Consciousness. It is so clear. I don't think that it will ever change. The approaches might change somewhat, whether leaning toward the conservative or a liberal emphasis, for example; but the basic philosophy will not change.

Two ongoing areas of so-called challenge to ISKCON, however, come from the ISKCON Reform Movement and from the figure of Narayana Maharaja,[6] and each in turn should be discussed here.

The ISKCON Reform Movement and the *ritvik* philosophy are perspectives that come from a position of being emotionally hurt. A lot of people who join ISKCON are basically idealistic. And when you see that a movement doesn't live up to your ideals, you get very hurt. This leads then to a very reactionary kind of philosophy. That's how I see the *ritvik* movement. Anyone who really knows Gaudiya Vaishnavism in terms of its history and philosophy knows that the whole *ritvik* idea doesn't have a leg to stand on.

Actually, some years back, the BBC was at our New York Ratha Yatra, the Festival of the Chariots, and they asked me about *ritvik* philosophy. At the time, I told them that it is basically just like deviated Christianity. You see, in the Christian tradition, certain adherents came to see Jesus as the only way, as a sort of God—this is actually a much later form of Christianity, a deviation, where Jesus is seen as a miniature godlike figure. Anyway, their view of Jesus is something akin to the way the *ritvik*s see Prabhupada—"Prabhupada is the only guru" is their cry. But this renders Prabhupada impotent, spiritually impotent—for, implicitly, it claims that he couldn't create anyone who could also function as a guru. And that's simply ridiculous. In the end, then, I stand behind what I said at that Ratha Yatra festival—*ritvik*ism is simply our Vaishnava version of deviated Christianity.

In terms of Gaudiya Vaishnava history and philosophy, the ISKCON Reform Movement to me is just an emotional reaction to being let down. Prabhupada was perfect, and that was the belief of everyone in ISKCON. So when the newly appointed gurus took over and it became clear that they were not perfect in the way that Prabhupada was perfect, everything else was seen as big failure, and Prabhupada was seen as the only

---

6   Bhaktivedanta Narayana Maharaja no longer represents a personal threat to ISKCON, as he passed away on 29th December 2010. Interestingly, as it is clear from Steven Rosen's comments in the interview, Rosen himself has never considered Narayana Maharaja to be a real source of opposition to ISKCON, and Rosen's comments about what may happen following his death in terms of the relationship between ISKCON devotees and disciples of Narayana Maharaja offer much food for thought.

legitimate guru. This is not the right way—to come to the conclusion that the 11 gurus, because they were not perfect like Prabhupada, were not gurus at all. No. This whole idea is fallacious.

All Vaishnava traditions include a concept known as *acharya purusha*—this is the main *acharya* to whom all other *acharyas* must bow down. In the Srivaishnava lineage, for example, the *acharya purusha* is Ramanuja. He is the overriding *acharya*. So, it is understood: all other *acharyas*, or great teachers, are subservient to him, and he is the central authority. In ISKCON, Prabhupada is clearly the *acharya purusha*. In other words, "regular gurus" don't necessarily have to be on Prabhupada's level. They can serve as initiating gurus, while Prabhupada, through his books and inspiration, will always be the major "instructing guru" for all of ISKCON. Thus, disciples get the benefit of a guru "in the flesh," who can guide them in practical matters, and also a high level pure devotee—Prabhupada—who is the last word in all matters of spiritual instruction.

Going back to the time of Lord Chaitanya, Narahari Sarkara Thakura wrote a book called *Sri Krishna Bhajanamrita*.[7] In that book there are instructions about what to do if your guru falls down. In principle, then, gurus can fall down. One of the big arguments of the ISKCON Reform Movement is that because the people who succeeded Prabhupada fell down they could not, therefore, have been gurus. That contradicts the whole idea of *Sri Krishna Bhajanamrita* since gurus *can* fall down, and there is a way to deal with that for a disciple. That's just a minor point in a way; there are many such points. So, if you look at it closely, the ISKCON Reform Movement is based on shaky philosophical grounds.

Coming now to Narayana Maharaja, this is a very different issue. Narayana Maharaja is a legitimate Gaudiya Vaishnava *acharya*. As far as I am concerned, there is essentially no philosophical difference between what he teaches and what ISKCON teaches. The differences are really institutional, not philosophical. There is, however, one philosophical difference: he says that one must have a pure devotee physically present in order to progress in Krishna Consciousness. This was not exactly the teaching of Srila Prabhupada, at least not in the way it is expressed in Narayana Maharaja's group. Please don't misunderstand me: the teaching is certainly there in the scriptures and in Prabhupada's books, that one needs the association of an advanced Vaishnava to progress in spiritual life. There is no doubt about this. But the exact way it is expressed,

---

7 Srila Narahari Sarkara Thakura, the author of the *Sri Krishna Bhajanamrita*, was a contemporary and close associate of Chaitanya Mahaprabhu.

nuanced, highlighted, and over-emphasised—this has a very particular history, and people should be aware of it.

I saw how it evolved that Narayana Maharaja started preaching this point, emphasising and highlighting it. He didn't preach like that initially. I knew Narayana Maharaja from before the time that there was a big controversy between him and ISKCON. I knew him from the early 1980s. His mood was very different then. He was encouraging and he wanted to see so many ISKCON devotees become initiating gurus. He was encouraging me to become an initiating guru and several of my other ISKCON friends also. He was not concerned with whether they were pure devotees or not. That didn't even enter the picture. If they were strong followers of Srila Prabhupada, they were fit to guide other disciples and help them go back to Godhead. But then what happened is that ISKCON leaders started to offend him, and he got very hurt. That pain that he felt at being rejected by ISKCON leaders affected the way that he preached about what is necessary. Then he would start to say that they were not legitimate gurus.

That's how all the problems began. That was the only difference between Narayana Maharaja's philosophy and ISKCON's philosophy. That aside, I myself have even encouraged people to go to Narayana Maharaja and to take instruction from him, and even to take initiation from him as well. I am truly a non-sectarian person. From my point of view he is a legitimate Gaudiya Vaishnava guru, and I would not at all discourage someone from taking initiation or guidance from him.

I should also say that Narayan Maharaja was always very kind to me personally. He took the time to answer my philosophical questions and treated me like his friend, albeit a very junior one. In some ways we were actually very close, and I had the highest regard for him, accepting him as a sort of shiksha guru or instructing spiritual master—not officially but in an informal sense. I was not a follower, as such, but he was always there when I needed him, and he was always ready to give me guidance.

The issue about having a pure devotee physically present at all times is fallacious, and if one thinks about the future it becomes clear why this is so. Just consider: when Narayana Maharaja leaves his body, which of his disciples is going to claim to be a pure devotee? And how are his followers going to agree? There's going to be in-house fighting. All his senior disciples are not going to accept one particular follower as a pure devotee. And then how will they progress? If their belief is that one needs a pure devotee always present to make advancement in spiritual life, what will they do when Narayana Maharaja leaves? This is the question.

I suspect that when Narayana Maharaja leaves his body his disciples will realise their untenable situation. Then there might be some harmony between ISKCON and Narayana Maharaja's group. I think that they will realise that they are basically in the same boat as the ISKCON devotees and maybe then will agree to work together. That, for me, is a distinct possibility that will happen in say 10, 15 or 20 years into the future. I can see how that will happen based on that one philosophical difference—that one must have a pure devotee present—the philosophical difference between Narayana Maharaja's movement and ISKCON. There could then be harmony in the future when Narayana Maharaja's group see that they are not all going to agree on who is the pure devotee.

Women and Gender Roles

I have high hopes for interrelationships between men and women in ISKCON. I was talking earlier about how Prabhupada had formed a monastic movement to establish the basis for his Society. But as the movement matured it became less of a monastic movement, and with that the equitable treatment of the opposite sex came into play more. Nowadays you can see *brahmachari*s or celibate monks treating women respectfully. The frustrations of the past are not there with the younger *brahmacharis*. They have made a commitment to celibate life, but that doesn't mean that they have to treat women badly or disrespectfully. As the movement matures the sexes will treat each other properly.

I think that women will have more leadership roles in the future. As they identify themselves as leading devotees, they will be engaged accordingly. That's already happened with the GBC and that will happen more so as the movement further develops. I have a very positive overall view of ISKCON and where it is going. ISKCON has grown as well as matured, and it will continue to do so.

Concluding Thoughts and Reflections

Finally, one important point that should be discussed and that involves me directly concerns ISKCON's interaction with the academic community. It's a very important development and something that Prabhupada wanted from the beginning. That's why he formed the Bhaktivedanta Institute. He wanted ISKCON devotees to be properly trained scientists so that they could show the truth of Krishna Consciousness in a scientific arena. Similarly, he wanted certain devotees to go back to school to get their PhDs in philosophy and religion, such as Ravindra Svarupa Dasa and Garuda Prabhu.[8] And Prabhupada always wanted scholars to appreciate the authenticity and legitimacy of his movement. That is why when scholars like Thomas Hopkins and Joseph O'Connell would come and visit the temple he would go out of his way to accommodate them, to give them time, to preach to them, and to give them *prasadam*. He considered it a very important aspect of his mission that it be widely accepted in the academic community. This is based on Krishna's own words in *Bhagavad Gita*: that whatever actions are performed by a great man, common men follow in his footsteps.[9] In that way what the educators and academics believe about ISKCON will filter down into the mass of people, and that will lead on to the common perception of ISKCON. So rather than saying ISKCON is a crazy cult, people will see it as a legitimate aspect of Gaudiya Vaishnava *dharma*.

Along those lines, in 1992 I started the *Journal of Vaishnava Studies*, engaging the research of academics from all over the world and publishing it four times a year. Now the *Journal of Vaishnava Studies* is considered the premier journal in the field of Hinduism. All major universities and research libraries around the world subscribe to it. Personally, I have devoted my life to sharing Krishna Consciousness with scholars, writing scholarly books and seeing to the ongoing publication of the *Journal of Vaishnava Studies*. I think that this is very important work. I am sure that other figures like Krsna-ksetra Prabhu[10] all know about the importance of academic involvement, as it is a key part of what ISKCON needs to contribute to the world.

But this invites critical reflection for ISKCON too, and I think that all of that is healthy. Let's take a topic such as "myth versus history," for example. It seems clear to me that ISKCON has more than enough legitimate history in areas other than those that might be debated. So debates around the search for the historical Krishna almost become irrelevant in the light of the clearly verifiable truths in the history of Gaudiya Vaishnavism. I am thinking in terms of Sri Chaitanya. When you talk about ancient history with stories of Krishna in the *Puranas*, scholars, of

---

8   Ravindra Svarupa Dasa (William H. Deadwyler) and Garuda Das (Graham Schweig) are initiated disciples of A. C. Bhaktivedanta Swami Prabhupada and are highly accomplished academically, both of them having distinguished publication profiles.

9   The full verse in the *Bhagavad Gita* Rosen invokes here is, "Whatever action a great man performs, common men follow. And whatever standards he sets by exemplary acts, all the world pursues." (*Bhagavad Gita As It Is* 3.21)

10 Krsna-ksetra (Kenneth R. Valpey) is an initiated disciple of A. C. Bhaktivedanta Swami Prabhupada, an ISKCON guru, and an established scholar. See also the interview with this devotee-scholar in this volume.

course, can question their historicity; but when you talk about Chaitanya and events that happened only 500 years ago, it becomes more difficult to paint the picture of a myth.

What I have found as the editor of the *Journal of Vaishnava Studies* does, in fact, bear out what I am saying here. I have befriended some 100 scholars from around the world who are not themselves necessarily involved in Krishna Consciousness or believers in Vaishnavism. But through their research they have come to legitimise Gaudiya Vaishnavism or Krishna Consciousness and the truth claims that one finds in the *Caitanya Caritamrta* and the *Caitanya-bhagavata*. It is truly remarkable to me and has increased my own faith as a devotee to interact with these scholars. For, although they are not necessarily believers, they have come to show from their research that Krishna Consciousness is legitimate and does embody a science of love of God.

A lot of readers of the *Journal of Vaishnava Studies* are also amazed at the truths that can be demonstrated by rigorous scholarly research. Those who know Sanskrit, Bengali and Tamil come forward and present their research in the journal, and it verifies Krishna Consciousness. So I think that this is wonderful, and I welcome also the challenge that it brings. People should come forward and try to disprove the truths of Krishna Consciousness. I think that the overriding result will be that the basic or fundamental truths of Krishna Consciousness will stand on their own. And the things that can't be proven, such as whether there really was a Ramchandra in Treta Yuga,[11] for example, is almost irrelevant to the overarching truths of Krishna Consciousness.

On another related point, take the claims of science about landing on the Moon. If someone, in fact, proved that we did land on the Moon, that would not disprove the truths of Krishna Consciousness. Prabhupada's basic point—and I was in the room several times when he would decry the Moon landing—was that we shouldn't have faith in material scientists. This is because they have the propensity to lie and to cheat. Sometimes just to get funding for their projects they manipulate the evidence. Prabhupada didn't want to put faith in these kinds of people. This is basically why he decried the Moon landing.

Further on this point, I was actually in the room with Prabhupada once when someone argued that they might have landed on the Moon,

11 In Hinduism, Treta Yuga is the second of four cyclical yugas or ages. It follows on from Satya Yuga, a period of perfect morality, and precedes Dvapara Yuga and Kali Yuga, the latter being the last of the four periods believed to be a time of irreligion and moral degradation. These four yugas or ages are held to span large periods of time, with the duration of Treta Yuga being 1,296,000 years.

and Prabhupada even said, "So they *did!*" He then said, "So what if they did? So what?" His point was that if someone is a non-devotee or if some-one is self-centred, then you can't really trust them; whereas if someone is pure and sincere and is developing the qualities of a God conscious individual, he is a trustworthy person.

I have spent considerable time with Sadaputa Dasa, and I have been with Svarupa Damodara Maharaj[12] where they have talked to scientists. And the scientists are very quick to realise that the things that they are questioning or criticising don't get to the heart of what Krishna Consciousness really is, and I have seen this also in my *Journal of Vaishnava Studies.* I interact with scholars all the time, editing their articles and so on. In this work we might come to the point where there is a truth claim that is questionable; but then the overarching point of the article is not about these peripheral truth claims. These points are usually incidental. The ultimate and overriding truths of Krishna Consciousness are verifiable, at least in one's own life, and that's what makes it a science.

---

12 Sadaputa Dasa (1947-2008), born Richard Thompson, has carried out research in the field of archeology. Svarupa Damodara Maharaj (1937-2006) — also known as Thoudam Damodara Singh — was the International Director of the Bhaktivedanta Institute for more than 30 years and promoted research on the relationship between science and Vedanta. However, the work of each of these ISKCON figures is controversial and problematic from a scientific perspective, according to Anna King in this volume. For criticism of them, see the interview with King in this book.

7. Interview With Joshua M. Greene

First Encounter

At age 19, in December 1969, I was a student at the Sorbonne in Paris studying comparative literature. On the Christmas break I went to London, visited the Krishna temple at Bury Place[1]—and came out of temple life 13 years later.

I was like many people my age, a product of the turbulent 1960s and the only child of divorced parents. I was cast adrift in those energised days and, like many other people, open to new experiences. The temple fit the bill quite well. It was exotic and exciting, and with the Beatles affiliation, it was gratifying from an ego perspective. Perhaps more significantly it involved a break with what the world had been up until that time. Moving into a Krishna temple represented the prospect of a new beginning, starting life again with an idealistic vision of helping respiritualise the world. The London temple was led by six senior students of A. C. Bhaktivedanta Swami Prabhupada: Yamuna, Gurudas, Shyamsundar, Malati, Mukunda and Janaki.[2] They took me under their wing and I doubt whether I would have entered on the path to becoming a Krishna *bhakta* had those six people in London not had been the caring, thoughtful, friendly, warm and compassionate human beings they were. I stayed because they represented the kind of company I wanted in my life.

When Prabhupada, the founder, first came West he had a vision of establishing a Western world counterpart to the institutional Vaishnava religion that had been started in India by his spiritual master, Bhaktisiddhanta Sarasvati Thakura. Prior to Bhaktisiddhanta there had never been an institution of Vaishnavism. Religion in classic Indian culture was lived and the world was your temple. British colonial missionary intervention required a response, and the response by the Bhadralok, the

1   Bury Place in Bloomsbury, London became the site of the first Hare Krishna temple in Britain on 5th June 1969, just six months before Joshua Greene took up residency there.

2   Bhaktivedanta Swami Prabhupada sent the three married couples (Gurudas and Yamuna, Shyamsundar and Malati, and Mukunda and Janaki) to the UK from America in 1968. They befriended George Harrison of Beatles fame and with Harrison's help were able to move into and convert Bury Place into a Hare Krishna temple.

Hindu intelligentsia, was to institutionalise Hinduism so that people had an option apart from Christian churches. Bhaktisiddhanta was the first to do this by creating the Gaudiya Math. Prabhupada was an exponent of that Math, and when he came to the United States in 1965 his purpose was to broaden the footprint of Vaishnavism. However, he was acutely aware that this was new territory, indeed very problematic territory. It was not like going to another city in India and opening a branch of the Gaudiya Math. He was dealing with hippies and other disenfranchised American youth; he was dealing with a country in tremendous conflict over the Vietnam War. So he presented Vaishnavism in a way that was appropriate to the time, place and circumstance.

To my way of thinking, Prabhupada always intended the Hare Krishna movement to grow and to be something more than a collection of temples. The core of his mission was to encourage *bhakti*, devotion to God, not as an institution but as a way of life. I'm speaking not as an official ISKCON representative, which I am not, but as an ISKCON supporter, as an individual who was fortunate enough to know Prabhupada and to travel and to spend time with him. I don't believe that Prabhupada's vision of the success of his mission was that the Western world would be running around with shaved heads or wearing *saris* and *dhotis*. I think his purpose, as stated in the original statutes, was to re-spiritualise a floundering civilisation. He wanted to bring people closer to God. And if some individuals chose to follow the cultural form that he represented, which is to say, shaved heads for men and *saris* for women, that's well and good. He had no objections to that. But I don't remember him ever insisting on it. So when speaking of the Hare Krishna movement, we have to define our terms here. There is the historic phenomenon of young people in the 1960s adapting, as I did in those days, to a very anti-establishment lifestyle. Then there is the movement as its founder envisioned it, and that deserves some clarification.

The young man I was in the 1960s—I think about him quite a bit. He was a well-intending fellow, insecure in many ways and certainly naïve about the workings of the world. What attracted him, an only-child baby boomer, was in part the ready-made family he found in temple life. Here were brothers and sisters all pursuing a common purpose. And there was an excitement in the notion of being invited to share knowledge that lived at the summit of the spiritual search. That is a very exciting prospect for a young person trying to establish a sense of identity and certainly not exclusive to the Krishna movement in the late 1960s; it's an excitement experienced by many people encountering transcendence for the first time, whatever its particular mode of expression.

Life is a mystery. We get up in the morning, our feet hit the ground, we grab our latté, and we are off and running. In the back of our heads—if we are at all thoughtful, thinking people—there is this nagging suspicion that there's more to it, that there's got to be more to life than just this. So encountering millennial wisdom, particularly on the order of a tradition as profound as Vaishnavism, can be a dramatically transformative experience. Remember the times. I had been to Woodstock. I had taken part in the anti-war demonstrations as editor of my student paper at the University of Wisconsin in 1968. I had been a part of peace rallies and marched with Martin Luther King. I had sung songs with Pete Seeger and gone to pop and jazz clubs in Greenwich Village where you could hear Bob Dylan singing five feet away from you and hear Jimmy Hendrix before he was known as Hendrix. Those were exciting times and there was a compulsion in those days to make something of your life. Krishna Consciousness presented the opportunity to do that—to turn people on to the idea that life is a spark of God, that we are more than our bodies and minds—that we are divine beings. This was a generation looking for peaceful alternatives to war. Well, here it was.

Changes, Developments and Future Prospects

Fast-forward, and there have been dramatic changes in the Krishna community over the past 40 or so years. No doubt the most important change is that a large number of people who jumped head-first into temples decided the time had come to grow up and take responsibility in the larger world. We had been part of an organisation that had its rituals and patterns of speaking and behaving, and moving the important part of that education into the larger world—that was a tremendously important change.

And a tremendously difficult one. Moving into the bigger world came with a lot of feelings of guilt, regret, remorse and bitterness. The thinking was, "Am I doubting the philosophy? Am I betraying my spiritual master? By moving out of temple life am I becoming a *karmie*, a materialist? Am I losing my own soul? Am I losing my Krishna Consciousness by saying that life within the institution is no longer sufficient?" That's the single largest change that seekers go through when the time comes to move out beyond the institution, and also the most valuable. The most meaningful contributions of faith communities in history have been made not by the institutional leaders but by the laity. The changes and innovations come from people who take their faith out into the world and do something with it.

That's where Krishna culture is now. The Krishna Consciousness movement today is a work in progress still, with a long way to go. I would describe the movement today as a place that is for me a source of joy and also sadness. Joy because I know what it represents, what it aspires to, and because it is an integral part of my life. Sadness because I know how far short of those aspirations it falls and because I know what it could be if devotees could shed the fear of stretching their muscles and thinking outside the orthodox point of view.

The more mature exponents of Krishna culture follow in the footsteps of those early devotees in London. They knew it would be a culture shock for me to move so quickly from the known world of New York and college into the unknown world of devotional life, and those wonderful people made that transition as comfortable as they possibly could. Continuing their protocol of serving people, of nurturing them in their spiritual life, I believe is at the core of Prabhupada's mission going forward.

I would say another important change is in vocabulary. We are of necessity having to learn to speak in a new voice. The language of Prabhupada's time is inadequate for effective communication today. I don't think it works to use his terminology such as "sinful activity," "*karmies*" "demons." Those terms may have had value in the nineteenth century, when Vaishnava faith was defending itself against conversional Christianity, but there is a kind of hellfire and brimstone background to those terms that today have no appeal at all. The job now for those who take their commitment to Vaishnava life seriously is to evolve a new language, a new vernacular that expresses the teachings of *Bhagavad Gita*, *Srimad Bhagavatam*, and other *bhakti* texts for the world we live in.

Times have changed, and so have the meanings of words. When the world was built of separate and distinct human groupings and nation-states, it was adequate to define a word such as *ahimsa* as "non-violence." As long as you did not commit violence to your own people, that was all that mattered. Whatever happened behind the borders of other countries was their own business. But the world has become a global village. What we do here affects people thousands of miles away. Particularly since the Second World War we have evolved notions of human rights and natural law. The notion of *ahimsa* today might be more accurately defined as "non-aggressive action," meaning a proactive intervention where the rights of others are being violated.

My point is that within *bhakti* there is a compulsion to act and to be involved in the larger society, and followers of *bhakti* have an obligation to take part in the healing and respiritualising of the larger world. Devotion must not be taken as a passive quality. It is not about my personal salvation but about the service I render to others. So there is this shift in vocabulary and also in an understanding of the concepts of devotional life. That is absolutely critical. To my mind that is at the top of the pile of what has begun now and what needs to be done in the years ahead.

We see this when we look at, for example, the work of Matsya Avatar in Italy.[3] He started the Bhaktivedanta Studies Centre, which offers state-accredited degrees in Indian art and culture and which looks at the impact of devotion on the Renaissance, on Enlightenment thinking, and on the world around us. That's one good example.

Another good example would be the work of Radhanath Swami in India. His social action programmes headquartered at the centre in Mumbai include a massive programme called Midday Meals, which feeds more than a quarter of a million indigent school children every day with hot, nutritious meals. His community has created mobile hospitals that perform cost-free cataract surgery. They have built one of the finest hospitals in the city. You can look at those practical examples of devotion in action.

Without wanting to toot my own horn, I try to do this in my own modest way through teaching. I teach in yoga studios, and my purpose is to infuse the yoga culture with a sense of its own philosophical roots and how yoga is to be practiced in the world. To my mind, the *Bhagavad Gita*, which is the single most important yoga text, is a treatise in psychology. Perfecting yoga and achieving a healthy psyche are on parallel tracks.

But moving on to public perception of Hare Krishna in North America, the most candid comment I can give about this is that I don't think there is one anymore. The worst possible thing has happened, namely, indifference. When one asks about a public perception it assumes that the public has one, and I don't believe it does today. There was a time going back 20 years perhaps when there was a public perception of the Hare Krishna movement in the sense that people felt accosted in airports, or read reports

3   Matsya Avatar Das (Marco Ferrini) is an initiated disciple of A. C. Bhaktivedanta Swami Prabhupada and in 1995 he founded the Bhaktivedanta Studies Centre (Centro Studi Bhaktivedanta) in Italy. The Centre is dedicated to the study and teaching of Vaishnavism and is a non-profit organisation recognized by the Italian government. Its Academic Department of Traditional Indian Sciences works in collaboration with several universities and colleges and attracts researchers worldwide. Its activities include conferences and residential seminars, and it has received accreditation from the Italian Ministry of Health. The Bhaktivedanta Studies Centre offers courses and seminars for firms on the Psychology of Leadership and well-being. Other courses developed by the Bhaktivedanta Studies Centre carried out in universities have also been certified by the Italian Educational Board for the training of teachers and lecturers at all levels.

of abuses, or saw devotees chanting in public. Devotees were a more visible part of the landscape of American culture previously. Maybe then one could say there was a public perception because Hare Krishna was in the news; it was on television; it was in the papers, for good or for bad.

Today, I do not believe that people who happen upon a Ratha Yatra festival,[4] for example, develop a "perception" of the Hare Krishna movement. I think that what they get is a Sunday festival that takes place, for example, here in New York where it is held each summer in Washington Square Park. There are some displays on vegetarianism and reincarnation, exhibits of artwork on the pastimes of Krishna from the *Srimad Bhagavatam* and other texts, stage performances of Indian music and dance. I think that people are certainly entertained by all of that. A rare few might take it seriously, enquiring more, asking, "Can you tell me more about vegetarianism? Can you tell me more about chanting?" And that is wonderful and truly an important part of the Vaishnava mission to bring awareness of spiritual concepts to the broader public. But there needs to be more, something deeper for thinking people to consider. One can ask, "If you love Krishna, what have done for Him lately?" And I think we have a long way to go there.

We need to be careful when talking of Hare Krishna as though there's a movement to be drawn into. That's not the case as it was, let's say, 30 or 40 years ago, when you were either "in" the movement or you were "out" of the movement, when you either lived inside a temple or didn't. There's a redefining of what it means to be a devotee and that is critically important. Who is the better Krishna devotee: someone who has received formal initiation from an authorised teacher in the Vaishnava lineage but who may not take that commitment very seriously, and whose devotional practices are lacklustre, and who doesn't do particularly much with it; or, on the other hand, someone who does not have any intellectual understanding of Krishna in Vrindavan but who is utterly given over, body and soul, to God and who lives such an inspiring life that other people are attracted to want to know more about God by seeing this person? Who is the better devotee?

So when it is asked, "Are people attracted to join the Hare Krishna movement?" I struggle with the question. It assumes that there is some

---

4   The annual Ratha Yatra festival (the festival of chariots) originated in Puri in the Indian state of Orissa and involves a street parade, using purpose-built wooden carts for the transportation of the images (*murti*) of Jagannatha (Krishna), Balaram and Subadra (Jagannatha's brother and sister). Prabhupada introduced this festival in the West and it is now performed every year in many major cities throughout the West. The festival also typically includes performances of Indian dance and music, as well as dramas celebrating the pastimes of Krishna as set out in Vaishnava scriptures.

kind of harvesting of souls, that the success of Prabhupada's mission is to be measured by the number of heads you can count at morning services; and I don't believe that. If you ask me, "What are the statistics on recruitment?" I don't have any to cite for you. I can't tell you, say, in the years 2008-2009 how many people visited a Krishna temple as a result of attending a Ratha Yatra programme or seeing chanting on the streets. Neither can I tell you how many people took up the chanting of the Hare Krishna mantra in the years 2009 and 2010. Because then you have to ask all kinds of other follow-up questions. I know yoga studios where people will sit around waiting on the *kirtan* singer Krishna Das, and they'll be chanting and swaying and swinging, and their arms will be rolling in the air; and the next day they go back to being whatever they were before. So, does that count? What are the barometers by which we are attempting to measure something invisible? The devotion of somebody's heart—how do you judge that? How do you quantify that?

But I am beginning to see—and continuing to see—a maturing on the part of those people who adhere to Vaishnava life. We are not running a contest. The world is in terrible shape. It needs thoughtful people to help put it back on track. We inch our way towards civilisation, and people who have a sense of the sanctity of all life have an important role to play, whether you want to call yourself a Krishna devotee or whether you want to call yourself a Christian, a Sufi or a non-believing scientist for that matter. I'm hoping to see this maturing process continue to a point where we stop judging people as either being "with" us or "against" us. I don't think that way of judging is healthy.

Indian and Non-Indian Devotees

When academics ask about the Hare Krishna movement as a modern religious movement, they have already branded it in sociological terms. That's a valid starting point for discussion, although not the only one. But given those parameters I am happy to offer comment on the growing presence of Hindus in Krishna temples.

First of all, I don't know too many people who define their core identity as Hindu. They may occasionally refer to themselves in that way since it is a convenient and common category for census forms, but they are human beings, and people attend temples for various reasons. Some of them who happen to be of Indian origin and whose family happens to be Hindu come to Krishna temples because it gives them some sense of familiarity. They grew up with it, they like the ceremonies and they believe in the deities. From childhood they have learned that you worship God, and a Krishna temple is a place to do that in.

One of the reasons why many people from India are drawn to Krishna temples is that Prabhupada and his followers have, without question, established the very highest level of deity worship. You will not find a more refined, elegant and authentic form of *archana* or deity worship than you find in Krishna temples. I believe that the religious Indian world is aware of that. So they come to take advantage of that opportunity. The concerns that some of my colleagues in Krishna Consciousness might express is that some temples have become dependent on donations from that Hindu portion of the congregation. That support may come with certain ritualistic strings, such as adding new holiday programmes or other features not introduced by Prabhupada. Are we, therefore, becoming a Hindu organisation? This is not what Prabhupada intended.

Sociologist Burke Rochford wrote a book that touched on this topic.[5] I was asked to write a review and felt obliged to comment on how he addressed this and other points.[6] I didn't find the description in the book adequately objective and felt that it skewed readers' impressions. It may be that in some temples, Hindus are happy with what is going on and in other places they are just part of the congregation. I haven't made a systematic study myself. But what is important for me here is the question: if indeed there is some risk of Krishna temples becoming Hinduised—going along with that kind of vocabulary—it's probably because there is a lack of imagination on the part of the people running temples when it comes to attracting a wider attendance. As a supporter of Prabhupada's society I have to admit that currently there isn't a whole lot of training going on within the Krishna Consciousness world that attempts to demonstrate the validity of its teaching in terms of application to larger challenges. I don't know too many people who are able to connect the dots between the *Bhagavad Gita* and climate change, for example. I don't know too many people who are effectively able to take Krishna's teachings and apply them to areas of armed conflict, poverty, HIV/AIDS, education, women's rights, children's rights, ecology.

There are some efforts, for example with Ranchor Prime[7] in London. He is doing some very effective work in ecology in Vrindavan. So there

5   Rochford, E.B., Jr. (2007) *Hare Krishna Transformed.* New York and London: New York University Press.

6   Joshua Greene's forthcoming review of Burke Rochford's book is to be published simultaneously in *ISKCON Studies Journal* and in the *Journal of Vaishnava Studies.*

7   Ranchor Prime was initiated by A.C. Bhaktivedanta Swami Prabhupada and joined the London Radha Krishna Temple in 1970. In 1987 he began working as an adviser

are some individual examples of where that work is being done. But with the majority of temples it's not on their radar screens, as far as I am aware. They are not attempting to make that leap from the tradition as it has been to date and the tradition as it might be in the future.

I do not believe that Vaishnavism as it has been historically is the same entity that it will be in the future for the simple reason that the world it lives in is not the same. For the first time in history we are in a globalised environment. That wasn't true even 100 years ago, let alone going back thousands of years in the history of Vaishnava culture. This is the first time in history that what you do here affects the lives of people halfway around the globe. That is why, to my mind, there is a compulsion within Vaishnava faith to move into the larger society and to become relevant. We are not relevant yet. For 99.99% of the world, we don't matter. Krishna Consciousness is irrelevant to most of the world.

Bhaktivedanta Manor is the largest Hindu pilgrimage site in the whole of the UK, but I don't think that you can extrapolate that to being an indicator of what role it might play in the UK 10 years from now. If things go as I would hope, there would be a much greater participation by non-Hindus at Bhaktivedanta Manor in another 10 years. By stepping outside the known and by taking the risk of moving into the unknown, it might be achieved. It involves stepping outside the safety zone of what we have been and of what the culture is supposed to look like and doing what the great *acharyas* have always urged us to do, and that is to take chances, to take risks. If someone really believes that this world is the universal form of God, the question is, "What are you doing to protect it?" And if you call yourself a devotee but do nothing to advance the community around you, well, in my book that would be called "impersonalism" or *mayavada* philosophy.

There is wonderful work being done by scholars such as David Haberman and Lance Nelson[8] in connecting *mayavada* philosophy to

---

to the World Wide Fund for Nature (WWF) on religion and conservation. His first book, *Hinduism and Ecology: Seeds of Truth* (Delhi: Motilal Banarsidass, 1996), arose from his work with the WWF in Britain and in India. This led to the founding of Friends of Vrindavan, an environmental charity for conserving the sacred forests of Krishna in India and strengthening the link between Hinduism and ecology. In 1996 he also helped found the Alliance of Religions and Conservation (ARC). He is the author of 12 books, including a comprehensive account of the early days of Krishna Consciousness in the UK: *When the Sun Shines: The Dawn of Hare Krishna in Britain* (Los Angeles: Bhaktivedanta Book Trust, 2009). His other major works include *Ramayan: A Journey* (New York: Welcome Rain, 1999); *Cows and the Earth* (London: Fitzrovia Press, 2009); and *Bhagavad Gita: Talks Between the Soul and God* (London: Fitzrovia Press, 2010).

8   David Haberman is a member of the Department of Religious Studies at Indiana University and spent the past two and a half decades doing research on the culture

the terrible state of the environment in India, for example. It's quite a compelling argument that, if you believe, as Sankara taught, that this world is like a dangerous ocean, filled with aquatic killer monster animals and our job is to get out of it, why on Earth would you want to get more involved in it? Why bother cleaning up the environment when this whole place is an illusion anyway? It's all *maya*, illusion. And that's a very popular idea, that when we achieve *moksha* then my ego dissolves, and this world of dreams disappears. Well, if this world is an illusion, why bother cleaning it up? Why would you bother fostering social action programmes if we are just meant to get out of here anyway? Why decorate a prison cell? Some of this thinking creeps into what might be called "salvationist Krishna Consciousness."

So if I am asked, "What would make it possible for Bhaktivedanta Manor not to be so Hindu or to have a wider representation?" I would say that the leaders there have to learn how to teach the philosophy in a way that emphasises its relevance to non-Hindus. In this sense, Vaishnavism has an extraordinary contribution to make to social action initiatives because we are the only ones—as far as I can tell—who have a perspective that says, not just from the point of view of the environment, not just from the point of view of being good people or creating a healthy future for our grandchildren, but from an ontological level of our very being, we are compelled to get involved in cleaning up the world. It is what we were made for. It is why we exist: to engage with God in an active level of devotion. This world is the arena for doing that. Here is where we act out our devotion. Here is where we learn to become true devotees of Krishna.

There was a time I remember in temples when anything other than distributing books or chanting was considered "mundane social work." That's what it was called: "mundane." We would say, "Look at those

of Braj. He has completed and annotated a translation of a sixteenth century Sanskrit text, *The Bhaktirasamrtasindhu of Rupa Gosvamin* (Indira Gandhi National Centre for the Arts, 2003), which focuses on the religious experience of *bhakti* in terms of classical Indian dramatic theory. Today he works in the field of religion and ecology, and he is on the Advisory Board of the Forum on Religion and Ecology based at the School for Forestry and Environmental Studies, Yale University. His current book project, entitled *People Trees: Worship of Trees in Northern India*, explores the conception of trees in the context of the tree shrines of northern India while reexamining such concepts as animism and anthropomorphism. He is also engaged in a project that investigates Western constructions of Hinduism with the aim of opening up the study of those regions of Hindu culture that have previously been ignored. Lance E. Nelson is based at the Department of Theology and Religious Studies, University of San Diego. He teaches courses in world religions and the religious traditions of Asia. Nelson has carried out research on Hindu religious history, concentrating on classical systems of Hindu theology and the relationship between Hindu religious practice and environmental concerns.

people. They don't know how to love Krishna so they open hospitals and distribute food." That was the attitude. There was a sense of, "Why do that?" Hopefully, we have now grown out of those immature days. The more we are able to articulate the connection between the world that most people live in and the world of devotion, the more that positive change will happen.

Theological Challenges: Conservative and Liberal Perspectives

It takes all kinds to make a movement. Conservatives play an important role. They are the guardians of the tradition. They are the ones who make sure that liberals like me don't get too far out of line. They are the ones who safeguard the integrity of the institution. They are the standard-bearers of the tradition. Conservatives are absolutely crucial to the health of a faith community. They are also the biggest impediment to its progress because by nature they will not step too far outside prescribed boundaries. That's not their job; they don't want to do it; and they shouldn't do it.

The liberals, on the other hand, are the ones who stretch the envelope and who make sure that tradition does not become so calcified that it cannot adapt to changing times. The liberals are the ones who evolve a new language, a new lexicon, a new terminology. So they play a vital role. The downside to liberals is that they can sometimes lack structure; and they can stretch things too far. Then you get a watering-down of the theology and it loses its power. I am constantly asking myself, "How far is too far?" So if you are a liberal, I would advise that you make friends with conservatives; and if you are a conservative I would advise you to make friends with liberals.

More importantly, we have to rethink assumptions about what ISKCON actually is. There seems to be an assumption that we are dealing with a fixed entity here, that ISKCON is a discrete world, defined as a certain number of buildings and properties that are owned by ISKCON Inc. of North America or Europe or described as certain temples and farms that exist in Asia; that there are certain communities in India and certain communities in Africa, and so on, and that all this constitutes ISKCON, the Hare Krishna movement. But there are problems with this notion of parameters. Most of the people I know don't live in temples. So whether liberals or conservatives are more in power in ISKCON today, it has no relevance to their lives whatsoever.

Moving beyond this issue, on to the ISKCON Revival Movement or schismatic groups, some of the people within those groups are quite aggressive. Some of them are just outright obnoxious. I have met some of them and I hope that I don't ever have to deal with them again. The ones I met were rude; they were presumptuous; and I don't have much good to say about them. That said, I have not met everyone within these schismatic communities. I don't know too many followers, for example, of Narayana Maharaja or Sridhar Maharaja, but some of those whom I do know are wonderful and I'm proud to call them my friends. It's pretty much the same with people within ISKCON: some are good friends, some are downright obnoxious. Institutional affiliations hardly define a person's character or value.

I think intelligent people are intelligent people, and silly people are silly people. Clearly mistakes were made. There were some tragic mistakes made by certain ISKCON officials towards some of the teachers from the Gaudiya Math, such as Sridhara Maharaja, and from other *maths* in India. There has been this holier-than-thou attitude that only Prabhupada has the way and everyone else is simply irrelevant and should be avoided at all costs. The view has been that they don't know anything anyway; so there is no point in going to them. That's childish and foolish and hurtful and just plain wrong. I don't see how people can hold their head up and think themselves to be a devotee of Krishna and yet be disrespectful toward others who have dedicated their life to Krishna. That escapes my understanding.

But if you are talking about those few individuals—and I'm assuming it's only a few—members of the IRM or ISKCON Reform Movement, individuals who are aggressively seeking to overthrow the ISKCON administration and assume ownership of the ISKCON properties and temples—that should certainly be stopped. That is not only illegal; it is immoral. If people have their own way of believing, that's fine. But why is it necessary for them to usurp someone else's place of worship? Why should you take over my temple in order to do what you believe? Where is the logic in that?

The IRM challenge is the view that the patient has a fever, so let's kill the patient. Not very good medicine. If some of them feel that ISKCON has gone astray and they really care about it, I would say, "Join the team. Let's work to make it better." It is a very naïve 1960s mentality that says in order to build a better world we have to overthrow the establishment; or we have to bring other things down before we can build something better. A more mature way of working for reform is working from within. The fact that the reform movement, as it is being called here, has decided that it has to break from ISKCON in order to reform it, I find unconvincing. And from some examples of people I know within that reform community I can comment that a lot of their bluster is really just a veneer over bitter feelings from having being mistreated in years gone by.

But it does need to be acknowledged and said that there were mistakes made. There were people in the ISKCON community who just behaved poorly. They abused others; they insulted them; they never knew how to honour the efforts of others in serving Srila Prabhupada's mission. So in that environment it is perfectly understandable that those people said, "The whole institution of ISKCON is finished. It's a waste. I can't work here. I have to go someplace else in order to express my devotion to Prabhupada."

Prabhupada himself did something similar, by breaking from the Gaudiya Math. But—and this is important—it was not until after he had tried, and tried, and tried, and tried again to get the Gaudiya Math to cooperate with him. They had all been charged by Bhaktisiddhanta to bring Vaishnava culture to the Western world. He was the only one who did it, and he asked them, "Please come and help me; let's do this together." Nobody did it until after he made it a big success. Then some individuals decided that they might be able to take advantage of his work after he passed away. That I find totally reprehensible. So I say again: "If you don't like something, help to make it better or just go your separate way. Why do you have to become antithetical and start lawsuits?" How is that behaving like a Vaishnava? In commenting here as I have done I am just expressing my own point of view, of course. I am not speaking on behalf of ISKCON. This is my own personal perspective.

Women and Gender Roles

When I first joined in December 1969, the question of gender roles would never have crossed anyone's mind. Such a question would have been considered silly. We were all devotees; we were all brothers and sisters. There was no question of distinction in terms of roles. There might have been some organisational distinctions or responsibilities: some people would do this; some people would do that. But it wasn't an issue. And that was very responsive to Prabhupada's demeanour. He never made those kinds of distinctions. He wanted us to be gentlemen and gentlewomen. He wanted us to be civilised. He didn't wish to see the hippie culture, if you will, come to characterise the Society that he had set out to establish. He really did try to civilise us and train us to be respectful of each other. So men should not hit on the women; and women should not attempt to seduce the men, and vice versa. He wanted us to be cultured and dignified representatives of the world of Krishna.

It so happens that the history of this particular effort, this particular Society, had a patch in time when a few very aggressive men acted on their understanding that what Prabhupada came to establish was a *sannyasi*-dominant movement, or institution run by senior men, and that women didn't really have a role to play other than the familial. And probably by dint of their force of character they were able to get their way—some pushy, A-type personalities who worked their way into positions of authority within the movement and, basically, put women down. Because they were preaching a kind of *brahmachari*- and *sannyasi*-dominant institution, women were left undefended.

So were children. Prabhupada begged us to care for and educate and nurture and love our children, but they, too, were often left unprotected. And the same question of inequalities could be applied to people of ethnic origin, to the roles of blacks and Hispanics in the Hare Krishna movement in those early days. There was a time when there was virulent bigotry in certain temples. I am talking now from the standpoint of my own experience, from what I have seen. The same lens can be pointed at Jews and other minorities. In that sense, ISKCON might have been a reflection of the same biases and prejudices that were going on in the larger society around it.

If you go back to the days of the 1960s and 1970s, there were no legal protections for women in the workplace, no sexual harassment laws; and blacks in parts of the South still could not sit with whites at the same table in a restaurant. There were cane beatings in schools sanctioned by state law. The fact that such prejudice was present in some parts of ISKCON is probably because ISKCON was an insular environment. I am not making excuses for those terribly hurtful behaviours. What I am saying is that I think it is a big mistake to isolate the crimes—and I'm going to intentionally call it *crimes* committed against women or children—and somehow make them endemic to a movement. Anybody who grew up in the 1960s knows that dysfunctional parenting was attributable to a lot more than just one religious community. It was part of the age, part of the larger culture.

Concluding Thoughts and Reflections

What people refer to as the Hare Krishna movement is an institution that represents the Vaishnava theology, the devotional perspective which is also called *bhakti*. It is at the very summit of Indian spiritual thought. It is also at the very summit of Christian thought; it is at the very summit of Jewish thought; it is at the summit of Islamic thought. It is the height of all mystic searching after God. The issue of ISKCON as an organisation attempting to represent that summit is one of trying to balance impossible elements, namely, the heart's yearning to know God and the value of having an institution within which to do that searching.

There is an old story: God turns to the devil and says, "I've got this really great idea. I think I'll call it religion." And the devil thinks for a minute and then says to God: "That *is* a good idea. Let me organise it for you." There is an imperative here. For those of us who have accepted the Krishna Consciousness way of life, there is an imperative now to be so confident in our own beliefs and to live that life so fully that we can step outside the familiar patterns of what it has looked and sounded like or what it has done in the past—and to consider a larger role in the bigger world. The mentality so far has been that we "owned the table," so to speak. We had the *truth* and others should see that. Moving forward now means to show some humility and gratitude for having a seat at the table along with other faith expressions. That means being so comfortable within our own faith structure—within our own knowledge and certitude that Krishna is God—that we can step outside that certitude to be part of a cooperative effort to heal the world.

I think also that scholars have a very serious responsibility to examine their own biases before they start to examine a faith community, whether it is the Hare Krishna world or any religious world. People look to scholars for an indication of the value of something. And if scholars paint too narrow a portrait of what the life of a Krishna devotee is, that can be a terrible disservice. There could be some extraordinarily important contributions to the progress of humanity—to the world around us—that would be compromised. This is because scholars will be perpetuating a biased view of Hare Krishna as a new religious movement, as a cult, or as some kind of historical phenomenon. There is certainly a historical quality to the Hare Krishna movement, but there is also an a-historic quality. The essence of the Krishna Society comes from outside historic conditions. The transcendent philosophy that lies at the heart of Krishna life is a gift to the world. That gift should be allowed to shine forth.

I do not blame other people for not inviting us to their party. I look to myself and ask, "Why am I not attracting more invitations to parties?" We have to learn what it is we have to say, what the contribution is that we wish to make. Then maybe people will start asking us to come and join them. It starts with listening. That's the very first principle—*shravanam.*[9]

---

9 *Shravanam*, Sanskrit for "hearing," is the first category of the nine processes of *bhakti-yoga* mentioned by Prahlada Maharaja in Canto Seven of the *Srimad Bhagavatam*, the other categories being chanting (*kirtanam*); remembering (*Vishnu*

It is the very first principle of devotional practice. And all these years we have thought that *shravanam* just means listening to ourselves. In terms of listening, I hope that ISKCON has learned to listen to others as well.

I find personally that I am most effective working with small groups of people. I am very happy doing that. People who come to my *Bhagavad Gita* sessions at the Jivamukti Yoga School here in New York come back because they have a good time. There is a sense of humour, and a sense of meaningfulness and openness to it that I also learn from. So if you give and take it always works.

My own spiritual master shed blood to build his Society. It would be devastating to see it somehow dissolve into some kind of ritualistic series of temples. That would be tragic. I fervently hope that is not the case.

---

smaranam); serving the Lord's lotus feet (*pada sevanam*); deity worship (*archanam*); praying (*vandanam*); executing orders (*dasyam*); serving a friend (*sakhyam*); and complete surrender (*atma nivedanam*).

8. Interview with Dr Edith Best

First Encounter

I had a friend in high school who invited me to visit the temple. That was in New York in 1973. But my first contact with the Hare Krishna movement was in 1969, also in New York. I was looking for a way to be spiritual 24 hours a day. I was always looking for spirituality, since I was four years old. That was when I first remember expressing that feeling. I had a desire to know God and to find spiritual perfection. Gradually, I wanted something where I could really be spiritual 24 hours a day. And I was very much convinced by the spiritual philosophy of Krishna Consciousness and the morning programme at the temple, so I was initiated. My first encounter with Prabhupada was in 1974. I was fanning him while he was speaking on the *vyasasana*, and then I got to meet with him in his room. I was very impressed, impressed that he was personal and authentic and caring.

Of course, the decision to dedicate my life to Krishna became the topic of discussion at home. My father carefully heard my story. He looked at me with the deep love of a relationship that is built on many frequent exchanges of shared conversation and adventures. "I'm so glad you are looking for God," he would say over and over. "I wanted to find spiritual truth when I was eighteen, but got distracted by marriage and business. I'm glad you are seeking a religious life."

My mother cried and cried. She couldn't see how naturally the path of my life led to this spiritual doorway. It would be many years before we became good friends and accepted each other's differences. For this impasse was not merely the result of her close-mindedness, as I liked to think. The fanaticism that affects many who first turn to a religious life made it difficult for me to approach her on some common ground. But Krishna was calling me.

Changes, Developments and Future Prospects

The three most important changes that have occurred in ISKCON, I would say, are how the movement is funded, understandings about succession, and our shift from a temple- or ashram-based organisation to a much broader society. Another important change is the availability of a large number of books, books which are not written and not translated by Srila Prabhupada, but which are also now informing our philosophy and practices. These include books published by the Bhaktivedanta Book Trust, books translated, for example, by Mahanidhi Swami and Bhanu Maharaj and books that other devotees have written, including books by Bhakti Tirtha Swami, Tamal Krishna Goswami, and Satyaraja Dasa.[1] In ISKCON originally, it was only Srila Prabhupada's books that were available, and this is not the case any more. This is a significant development because it means that new devotees can and often do read a lot of those books before they really know Srila Prabhupada's books. So it's not as easy nowadays to find people who have a really good sense of Srila Prabhupada's mood and mission.

But the Hare Krishna movement itself offers a platform for spiritual perfection. It offers society and association to help its individual members attain spiritual perfection and it brings spiritual knowledge and practices to the world. This has always been the case and this has not changed. This is the essential purpose of the Hare Krishna movement. Its function is to provide a platform or place or structure for individual and collective spiritual growth.

When it comes to public perceptions of the Hare Krishna movement, however, I think that you have to look in different parts of the world. Public perceptions are very different in different parts of the globe. In some parts of the world people may not even know that we exist. In other parts of the world we may be seen as a cult. In the UK we have done a lot of work to identify ourselves as the epiphany of Hinduism; so I guess that a lot of the public see us that way there. I don't know if attempts at portraying ourselves as a group have been clear in saying that, rather than devotees being Hindus, Hinduism is Krishna Consciousness. We've tried to redefine Hinduism. Has that translated into the public's perception? And would this apply equally well, for example, in France? I doubt it. This because there hasn't been that kind of propaganda in France. Again, would that apply well in America? Definitely not. And this is because in America the view about the place of religion is different. We have the separation of church and state in America, and there just hasn't been any

---

1   These influential figures in ISKCON have been responsible for the production of a large corpus of texts. The translation of key Vaishnava works and other books authored by Mahanidhi Swami and Bhanu Maharaj number some 30 volumes. Bhakti Tirtha Swami alone has authored 17 books. Before his demise, Tamal Krishna Goswami was trustee of the Bhaktivedanta Book Trust and has also written widely on various religious topics, including two classical Vedic dramas. Satyaraja Dasa is the author of over 30 books published in numerous languages.

attempt by the movement's leaders there to position the Hare Krishna movement as being the voice of Hinduism. Therefore, public perceptions are going to be very different. Then again, they are going to be further different in different parts of America itself.

In London, devotees are out on the streets at least three times in a day. But in other places or in other parts of the world that is not the case. I noticed one thing when I lived in North Carolina. There was a big devotee community there. We were often out in our devotee clothes and people didn't pay much attention to us. But if I went to a town that was an hour away where devotees were often not wearing their devotee clothes, then I got a lot of stares and a lot of people not knowing who I was and how to deal with that.

When I was studying at university I found that people were very respectful. They didn't really know much about me or what I was; so they tended to ask me questions in the last class on the last day of the semester. But that's the university environment where people are trained to be open to multiculturalism and to be tolerant. Does that represent the public perceptions of the people in general? Probably not. Clearly, then, public perceptions of the Hare Krishna movement are very different in different places and in different settings.

On the topic of ISKCON's future or recruitment of new followers, no one really knows what will happen, and it's no longer really that important to me. However, I sometimes present it as if it is important to me because I see that other people think that it is important to them. So I might use it as a way to motivate people's interest; but it doesn't really have any importance to me. I don't think anyone in ISKCON is capable of answering questions about this.

Chaitanya Mahaprabhu's movement is predicted to exist for 10,000 years.[2] What role ISKCON will play in that or to what extent ISKCON will exist as a spiritual organisation, I just don't know. ISKCON has changed so much in the last 30 years. I could never have predicted 30 years ago—and nor could anyone else either—just what kind of changes there would be. We don't know what kind of societal changes there are going to be outside of ISKCON; nor do we know which part of ISKCON is really going to be directing the changes inside the movement. But my

---

2   In the *Brahma-Vaivarta Purana* (Fourth Part: "Krishna-Janma-Khanda," chapter 129, verses 50-59) one reads that Lord Krishna foretells that, after 5,000 years, the chanting of His names would spread all over the world, beginning a 10,000 years Golden Age period. In ISKCON it is believed that the Golden Age began with the advent of Lord Chaitanya in 1486 and that the movement Chaitanya established took a leap forward when Prabhupada himself began spreading Krishna Consciousness around the world.

happiness comes from the fact that I see ISKCON as a spiritually vibrant organisation at present. What ISKCON's role is or what my own role is here is something I don't really need to know. I am a little soldier in the army. It's the generals who know, but they don't tell me their plans. And by "the generals" I mean God; I don't mean the GBC. They don't know either.

Indian and Non-Indian Devotees

There are two main reasons why we have Indian Hindus involved in the Krishna Consciousness movement. One reason is that non-Indians don't have a lot of children. Religious organisations to a large extent have to grow through their children. So we are tending to grow through the children of the people who are closest to our organisation: the Indian Hindus. The other reason why we get a lot of Indian Hindus—and the sociologists would know about this principle—is because of the conservation of *cultural capital*.[3] For Indian Hindus to join ISKCON means that they can still draw upon much of their cultural capital. Whereas for the non-Indians their own cultural capital becomes essentially useless, and they have to learn everything anew, including learning a new vocabulary, a whole new set of scriptural and historical personalities, new scriptures, and new ways of behaving. So it is much easier for us to attract members of the community that shares a lot of our cultural capital. This is the reason, along with the other reason mentioned, why we have a large influx of Indian Hindus.

But, importantly, it depends on where you are in the world. There are certain parts of the world where there just aren't many Indian Hindus, such as Russia, Poland and Hungary. They just don't exist in large numbers in those places. So there is the question of whether all this is relevant

---

3   *Cultural capital* is a term that has gained widespread use in academic circles since it was first coined by the French sociologist Pierre Bourdieu. In Bourdieu's work it refers to types of social asset or privilege that are non-financial in form and which may be used as a means of exchange to gain social status or social honour. As such cultural capital may be found or expressed in a variety of domains, for example, in intellectual, in educational or in religious life. Edith Best's generalised use of the concept simply highlights how the religious knowledge and cultural heritage of Indian Hindus enables them readily to achieve spiritual meaning and benefit in the world of Krishna Consciousness. By the same token, Best indicates that for Western devotees it is much harder for them to achieve the same sense of spiritual value or meaning, as it requires them to learn a new way of thinking and a new set of practices that are essentially culturally alien. For Best, then, this principle helps to explain why many Indian Hindus, as opposed to non-Indian devotees, are drawn with ease into the Krishna Consciousness movement.

to them. If you are in the UK, for example, you are going to think that ISKCON is being taken over by the Indian Hindus. But if you were in Poland, the question would not even arise. Even when thinking about the actual effect Indian Hindus may have, it really does depend upon the place itself. In some cases the ISKCON centre becomes Hinduised, but in other cases the Hindus become ISKCONised. And in many places there is some mix of the two patterns. So you have a lot of ISKCONised Indian Hindus and you also have some Hinduisation of some ISKCON centres. Some centres really have become Hinduised, where the deities we are worshiping, where the songs that we are singing, where the festivals that we are observing are just not what Srila Prabhupada established. That is, they are part of broader Hinduism. So here our cultural behaviour and our superstitions become clearly Hinduised.

Yet I have been in some centres where the Indians form the vast majority of the congregation and I have seen that they have become ISKCONised. Here their way of thinking, their culture, and their behaviour have changed to being practically the same as that of the Western devotees. And I see the benefits of the Hindu Indian participation. To a large extent, Indian Hindus who have been brought up in Western countries are like the *gurukulis*, the children born to ISKCON members, embodying a combination of Western and Eastern cultures in their own upbringing and in their own bodies: it is part of them. Being both a Westerner and an Indian spiritualist is their own personal identity. I see this both with the Indian Hindu children who have been brought up in the West and the children of the other devotees. They both have that mix that they bring; so they personally exemplify what we want our movement to do.

The older members of the Indian community—not the younger generation brought up in the West—tend to be much more moral and stable than members from outside of India. They still have the ethical and moral values that existed in the West before the 1970s, particularly in terms of the family. Divorce, for example, started to be accepted in the West in the 1970s. This is now changing very rapidly, and it is changing even more rapidly outside India. But if you look at Indians you see that they are bringing a lot of moral stability to ISKCON. They tend to bring much more ethical standards and are much more responsible people. They tend to have more responsible careers; whereas there has been a tendency amongst many Westerners who joined ISKCON to have the view that Krishna Consciousness means not having a regular job and not having any kind of regular income. Therefore, the Indian Hindus tend to bring moral, ethical and financial responsibility and stability to ISKCON. But the moral and ethical advantage seen in Indians seems now to be decreasing, both in and out of India. In another 20 to 40 years, that advantage may be gone.

A disadvantage certainly is that Indian Hindus can introduce non-Gaudiya Vaishnava trends. They are bringing in Hindu behaviour, Hindu food and Indian ways of thinking that vary. And, of course, Hinduism itself is varied. People in south India, people in Gujarat and people in Bengal are bringing in very different traditions. They are bringing in practices that look like Krishna Consciousness but are not that. Westerners also bring in their own culture and thinking that is different from Krishna Consciousness. There is much of the New Age that is brought by Westerners into the Hare Krishna movement. This is not a problem to identify. But when something comes into the movement via the Indians, it becomes much harder to recognise. Clearly, then, in some cases there has been a real merging or mish-mash of practices.

Yet another problem with having very many Indian Hindus is that Hinduism was traditionally something like the religion of the Amish people, where the religion is what you are born into, a religion that does not seek converts. Hindus see themselves as an ethnic group. And when you have a lot of ethnic Hindus in one place, people who are not of that ethnic group and who come to that place may perceive Krishna Consciousness as an ethnic religion, and choose not to become involved. This is the big problem that we have in London. However, I have also run into this problem in Wellington, New Zealand.

On all these matters, you have to take the work of sociologist Burke Rochford cautiously.[4] First of all, he is a very good friend of mine, but he has researched the Hare Krishna movement in America. This really has to be kept in mind because America *is not* the world. The situation he describes for America does not exist in every place. Even in America it's not all the same. I am in Hawaii, and there is no Indianisation of ISKCON here. There are not many Indians in Hawaii to Indianise it. It's the same elsewhere, for example with Puerto Rico in the Caribbean. I was there in 2001, and there were maybe only five Indians who would come to the temple because Puerto Rico doesn't have a large Indian population. So it all depends on where you are. If you are in Toronto then the temple seems to be all Indians. But this is not true everywhere else. It certainly is not true in Alachua, which is our biggest Hare Krishna community in

4   Best has in mind Rochford's recent book publication on the Hare Krishna movement: Rochford, E.B., Jr. (2007) *Hare Krishna Transformed*. New York and London: New York University Press.

America. Also, I was recently in San Diego for Gaura Punima,[5] and here I would say it is around one-third to one-half Indians. I was in New Jersey in 2002-2003 and there I was one of only five non-Indians at a festival. There were some 600 people there but only five non-Indians.

I would therefore say that Burke Rochford is relying too much on certain select places. He is also relying too much on people who perceive ISKCON as being dominated by Indians. He is not seeing the whole picture. If you go out of America it is completely different. I have already mentioned Russia. There are hardly any Indians there. The government does not allow them in. There are 7,000 Indians in the whole of Moscow; and we get 40,000 people at our Janmashtami festival in Moscow—40,000 people, and they are mostly not Indians. Our biggest festivals outside India are in the Ukraine and in Russia, where we have thousands of people at all the festivals. We might see two or three Indian faces. But we are just not getting many Indians there. In Hungary it's the same picture, and there we get tax money from the government and their universities come and do research on us. So what are we talking about here? You have to look at the different places where the Hare Krishna movement is found. And the effect of the Indians in a particular place really depends on how the local leaders deal with the Indians.

As I have already pointed out, where an expanding number of Indian Hindus are coming in they tend to bring their customs and values into the organisation of ISKCON. So even if you go to Russia, where there are hardly any Indians, much of ISKCON Russia has been affected by Indians in ISKCON generally. Because many Russians go to India, and because a lot of the devotees who preach in Russia are connected by the Indian influx, you will find that there are some trends here and all over the world that have come from the fact that there are a lot of Indians in broader ISKCON. When Prabhupada was with us there was a very small number of Indian Hindus in ISKCON. So now they are bringing some of their village customs and values, but most of them, as I have said, are values of hard work, responsibility and respectability. And most definitely the fact that a large portion of our worldwide movement involves the Indians makes us a much more mainstream and respectable organisation. We are seen that way more and more.

Indians, of course, bring in a lot of money and volunteer labour. Again, however, it all depends on where you are based. But the places that

---

5 Gaura Purnima (literally, "Golden Full Moon") is a Gaudiya Vaishnava festival held in ISKCON centres throughout the world. It occurs in the month of March (Chaitra) and celebrates the birth or appearance day of Chaitanya Mahaprabhu who in ISKCON is held to be an incarnation of Krishna and Radha combined.

don't have a large Indian population as part of ISKCON, as in Italy, for example, are having a lot more trouble getting people to volunteer money and labour. Part of Indian culture means that when you go to the temple you give a donation. This is not so much a feature with the non-Indians. It is also part of Indian culture that you go to the temple and offer some service. This is a little harder in the case of the non-Indian devotees.

Turning to groups like the Pandava Sena, this is an incredible organisation. It's very much active in the UK but not so much so in other parts of the world; and it serves almost entirely the Indian youth who were born and raised in the UK. Some children born into non-Indian devotee families are involved in it, though it is primarily for Indian youth who have been brought into contact with ISKCON while growing up. The Pandava Sena gets the youth very much involved as volunteers in the service of Krishna Consciousness; and they organise their own programmes.

But members of the Pandava Sena do have problems when they get older, when they marry and move out of their family homes. Then they become less active in ISKCON, less active than they were when they were younger and single. Yet it is a very dynamic organisation, and I see the Pandava Sena as giving a lot of hope in terms of the spiritual vitality of ISKCON.

As far as the *gurukulis* are concerned, they are a very diverse group. There was a time when it was possible to put the *gurukulis* into one category. It meant simply somebody who had attended an ashram school. But it is really not a monolithic group any more at all. Now it has generally come to mean anyone whose parents are devotees. The growing-up experience of children in ISKCON crosses a huge spectrum today, from parents who teach their kids practically nothing about Krishna Consciousness, and some of them going to non-devotee schools, to children going to an ashram *gurukula* who receive very intensive training in Krishna Consciousness.

The effect of the *gurukulis* on ISKCON is also varied. Sociologists hold that children born into the movement are more likely to leave than converts, and are also more likely to have lower standards of strictness. And we can actually see that happening amongst our *gurukulis*. While they consider themselves to be devotees, they do have a tendency not to follow even the most basic austerities. They then see themselves as devotees simply because they believe in Krishna and have attended a *gurkula*. This can definitely be observed.

You can also detect awareness among ISKCON leaders, wanting to engage the children of devotees in service and in leadership positions, as well as seeing them as valuable members of the Society. Previously, they were only seen as valuable members of the Society if they were strict. This is not really the case anymore, although there are still some leaders who say that the children of devotees are useless unless they are really strict.

With the Indians, as I have already indicated, the children embody a mixture of cultures. They have a mix of Western and Indian cultures—unless they have been brought up in India to Indians in an entirely Indian community. Where the children of Indian devotees have been raised in a non-Indian culture, they have the ISKCON culture plus the outside non-Indian culture, and this is something the converts do not have.

However, I see that we are not training or engaging the children of the devotees well. We don't encourage devotees to have children and, if they do, we don't encourage them to have many children. We don't really have the facilities to train our children. Outside of India we have practically no schools. In all of North America we have only four schools, two in the same community; in all of Europe we have three schools, two of them in London; in the whole of Australia we have only one school; in the whole of New Zealand there is also only one school. In Russia we don't have any schools at all. In 2005 we had five schools in Africa but they have all since closed. So we still don't really make an effort here.

We equally don't really have any organised way to produce material for our children. We have a big publishing house to produce adult literature. If you want to produce any literature for children, you have to do it on your own. There is nothing within the organisation of ISKCON to support you in this in terms of money or manpower or facility. There is nothing in place to support schools. There is no school system. The Ministry of Education in ISKCON is just starting to think about someday possibly having a support system in place. They are starting the discussion and the planning.

So we just have not understood the value of our children. And I think that our children have a very odd situation, where it is hard for them to find a place in the movement. If you are, say, 20 years old and you have been brought up nicely as a devotee—which doesn't happen so much anymore—but if you have nevertheless been raised nicely, then you are living as a 20-year-old devotee, a spiritually mature person in ISKCON, but are not treated like that. And if you then associate with other 20-year-old devotees, they will typically be converts who are on a very different level spiritually, psychologically and socially. If, alternatively, you associate with devotees who are on the same level of spiritual maturity as yourself, they will all be middle-aged or old people. It is then really hard for you to find a place. This is starting to change but the movement still doesn't really accord young devotees the respect that they deserve. They are not seen as the important resource that they are. The point that I often make to others is that a 20-year-old who has been raised in the movement has the wisdom of an older person but the idealism and energy of youth. But generally people have one or the other—idealism and energy or maturity. The leadership is starting to have the idea, at least in theory, that we should be taking advantage of that; however, it's not very pronounced just now.

Theological Challenges: Conservative and Liberal Perspectives

Conservative and liberal views exist in every organisation. They will always exist. As my friend Braja Bihari Dasa taught at Bhaktivedanta College in 2010, it is polarity to be managed rather than a problem to be solved. What I see increasingly in ISKCON is that there are leaders and/ or centres that are situated on one or the other end of the conservative-liberal spectrum. And different devotees find their own places where they can be comfortable. Apart from extreme ends of the conservative and liberal divide, I think that it is mostly a false dichotomy, however. A vibrant organisation has to move along the conservative-liberal continuum in order to respond to different situations. But if there is a real difference between liberalism and conservativism, it is the lack of consensus between what counts as a principle and what is viewed as a detail. Different people have different opinions about that. If what I think is a principle you think is a detail, then I'll call you a liberal. This is because you would be altering something I don't think should be changed. And if what I think is a detail you call a principle, I'll call you a conservative because you are holding onto something that I think should be changed. And it is very rare in ISKCON that you will find two people who will agree on what is a principle and what is a detail in every respect.

I have found some devotees who are extreme on the conservative-liberal continuum. An extreme liberal, I would say, is someone who labels almost everything as a detail; that is, one whose list of principles is very small. At the conservative end of the spectrum, this would be someone who labels almost everything as a principle and whose list of details is very small. Sociologically speaking neither of those positions is healthy for the continuation of the organisation. The conservatives may think that they are keeping the purity intact but really, if they are not willing to adjust, then they are likely to destroy the organisation. But I actually think that there is enough variety in ISKCON at the present time and that this variety is healthy. Everyone in the organisation should now be able to find their place. One major theological or philosophical shift that has occurred is in our understandings of succession. When Srila Prabhupada left this world in 1977, decisions and resolutions on how to continue the disciplic succession of guru and disciple were made on the basis of management, practicality, and expediency. Unfortunately, ISKCON leaders did not declare a moratorium on initiation while they researched guru, *sadhu*, and *shastra* for how the succession of guru and disciple could continue.[6] Problems with the first system—serious problems—surfaced within a short time, and since then various systems have been tried or adjusted in over a dozen ways on the same principles of management, practicality, and expediency. When there is a suggestion, as was made by the Shastric Advisory Council to the GBC, that ISKCON return to the succession system which guru, *sadhu* and *shastra* explain, the general response from leadership is that ISKCON must do things differently on account of being an institution. Since ISKCON claims to gain its spiritual authority from its disciplic succession, how can it continue as a spiritual institution if the very basis of succession is not grounded in its own tradition? And, surely Prabhupada knew that ISKCON is an institution, and would have many times explained how adjustments to the tradition of succession were to be instituted if he deemed them necessary. On the contrary, Prabhupada only explained succession as it is in the scriptures and the tradition of saints. The elements of succession that are not in accord with guru, *sadhu* and *shastra* include how a person decides to take up the service of initiating, how a person chooses a guru, how a guru chooses a disciple, and how a disciple deals with a guru who falls from the standard.

I would say that unless our understandings of succession are in tune with our tradition it will mean straying away. This is *the* major problem, *the* major concern. It represents a danger for ISKCON. I am personally

---

6   In ISKCON one frequently cited statement on the doctrine of *guru, sadhu* and *shastra* is where Prabhupada writes: "We have to understand...God by the instructions of authorized persons...*sadhu-shastra-guru*: one has to test all spiritual matters according to the instructions of saintly persons, scriptures and the spiritual master. The spiritual master is one who follows the instructions of his predecessors, namely the sadhus, or saintly persons. A bona fide spiritual master does not mention anything not mentioned in the authorized scriptures. Ordinary people have to follow the instructions of *sadhu, shastra* and *guru*. Those statements made in the *shastras* and those made by the bona fide *sadhu* or *guru* cannot differ from one another." (*Srimad Bhagavatam* 4:16:1 Purport) Edith Best holds that it is this very doctrine which has not been appropriately adhered to or clearly worked out in ISKCON and which is still a major challenge and ongoing concern for leaders of the Hare Krishna movement.

convinced that ISKCON is not engaged in the succession of authority in line with our tradition. I see this as being very dangerous, but others in the movement might see it as a mere detail. There are problems with how devotees take initiation; how someone becomes a *diksha* guru or a *siksha* guru; how someone becomes authorised to become guru; how a disciple chooses a guru; how a guru chooses a disciple. The way these are all taking place in ISKCON is not in accordance with our ancient tradition. All this is not happening according to our scriptures or according to Gaudiya Vaishnavism. It's not happening according to what Srila Prabhupada put in place. So all this is not according to guru, *sadhu* or *shastra*. It is basically something that has been made up.

Devotees in general have to understand what these three things are. I would say that most devotees don't even know what guru, *sadhu* or *shastra* are in ISKCON in relation to these questions. Devotees have to learn that it is important that these three things are in harmony. We need to provide a schema in ISKCON for implementing the guru, *sadhu* and *shastra* plan for succession. I am doing some study myself about how to bring change, how to bring change in organisations, and how to influence people in organisations.

Now, with the IRM or with Narayana Maharaja—schisms are inevitable and bring competition. In general the competition has been very helpful for ISKCON. First of all, such organisations siphon off difficult, discontented, trouble-making people and in this way are doing ISKCON a very valuable service. Another important point is that they tend to provide perspectives that are useful to ISKCON as an organisation, perspectives that then come into ISKCON itself. So with both the two groups mentioned, a lot of their philosophy and practices have been brought into ISKCON. With the IRM, there has been much emphasis on Prabhupada as the central guru of ISKCON. Before the IRM emerged there was a strong idea that your individual *diksha* guru was your only authority. There was not much talk about Prabhupada being everyone's *siksha* guru.

Because of the Narayana Maharaja group there is also now in ISKCON much more emphasis on inner development of *bhakti*. Overall, this has been positive for ISKCON. But it would have been a lot better if ISKCON had provided devotees with what they needed in their own home, as it were. A friend of mine once said that if you have to go outside your house to get what you need, then you have to associate with people who are not like-minded. So if ISKCON does not offer what devotees need and they then have to go outside for this, this is not a happy situation. However, it's inevitable in a way. I don't think that you can stop it. But the idea that these groups might draw so many devotees away and be a threat such that

ISKCON may in the future not exist anymore is silly. And in terms of ISKCON's purity, how could they really be a threat? What do these other organisations have to do with ISKCON's internal purity or its stability? I don't think that they are a major threat at all. There is no danger whatsoever of ISKCON members somehow all running off to join some splinter organisation.

What I see actually is that all the splinter groups want recognition from ISKCON. It is the splinter groups who care about recognition from, and being accepted by, ISKCON. But ISKCON does not care one fig about getting recognition from them. ISKCON's leadership does not really care if the leaders of the Narayana Maharaja group, for example, say that ISKCON is a *bona fide* organisation. ISKCON leaders were irritated and amused when Narayana Maharaja said in 2009 that everybody in ISKCON is an insincere money-grabber.[7] Yet ISKCON's *bona fide* status is not dependent on Narayana Maharaja certifying it. ISKCON is *the* big organisation. None of the splinter groups comes close in terms of size and influence, and the majority of them probably will not exist at all past one or two generations of followers. They are far too small.

Women and Gender Roles

Within ISKCON, there are some places where men and women have roles that are consistent with what Prabhupada taught and did, and in other places women are simply like pieces of furniture. I was in one particular temple recently where there were 150 men attending the morning programme and 10 women. As soon as the *kirtan* was over, for *japa* time, the women's *japa* time was spent in a corner behind a barricade. So the men had the whole temple and the women were in a corner, a really bad place to chant because you couldn't walk, and everything that was surrounding you there was unattractive. None of the local women chanted there, not one. The only women who were chanting there were guests. Although I was invited to that centre by the management to hold seminars, they wouldn't let me give the seminars in the temple room. That is one example of one particular centre.

But then if you go to a place like Radhadesh in Belgium it is all very different. I would say that this, from my experience, is equal to what I've heard about Alachua. In Radhadesh there is a system and a situation that

---

7   The negative comment attributed here to Narayana Maharaja is one that is frequently encountered throughout the global ISKCON community, one which underscores the history of tension that has long existed between ISKCON members and the schismatic leader Narayana Maharaja.

is very much like how ISKCON was when Prabhupada was directly running it, before his disciples did the majority of the management. The gender roles in Radhadesh exemplify that. But I haven't seen that standard in too many other places.

Again, everything here is on a continuum. It really does depend on where you are. I would say that overall in ISKCON the situation is improving in terms of gender roles, going back to the tradition. But there are some groups that are really fighting to keep women from being recognised as far as possible in ISKCON. They are making a lot of propaganda; they are making a lot of noise; they are doing a lot of threatening; they are making a lot of political moves; and sometimes they make legal moves, too. Will ISKCON split along these lines? Some devotees say it will. But I hope not.

Again, as I have said, it all depends on the location where you are in ISKCON. Impressions of the roles of women in ISKCON will change radically in the UK, for example, as you go from Soho Street to Bhaktivedanta Manor. Women have much more active roles in the Soho Street morning programme than they do at the Manor.

Now, within the GBC there are resolutions that have been passed because of pressure from the Women's Ministry, but those resolutions are simply not applied in some ISKCON centres. It is not as if going through the bureaucratic structure necessarily makes a change in the culture and practices of ISKCON. It might; then again it might not. It depends on where you are and who is in charge and if those in charge decide to follow it. You can't say, "Prabhupada did this or it's a GBC resolution; so why aren't you doing it?" They'll just say, "Because we don't want to." Then if you go back to the GBC and ask, "Why are they not following this?" They will then say, "We can't do anything about it." But this happens in every area of ISKCON, not just the one relating to women.

Our administrative structure is what we call in managerial terms "loosely coupled." Overall, I happen to think that it is a very good structure. This is because I feel that if ISKCON were run in a more bureaucratic manner, the spirituality would all be stopped. So I am happy, overall, that large portions of ISKCON can operate with their members thumbing their noses at GBC resolutions. The problem, however, is that when the GBC does something good it also doesn't have much of an impact.

In terms of women being gurus or taking *sannyasa*, I would say that there are possibilities for the first but not for the second. Prabhupada specifically forbade women from taking *sannyasa*.[8] However, we do have

---

8   On this matter Prabhupada says, "A woman is not supposed to take *sannyasa*. So-called spiritual societies concocted in modern times give *sannyasa* even to

quite a number of women living like *sannyasis* without the title, without the saffron robes. For example, I know one ISKCON lady who is basically a *de facto sannyasi* and who would really like for there to be some regulation of her status. She would like for there to be some established service for renounced women like her because she feels that she would get the respect and the help that she needs. But I say to her, "Right now you can do whatever you want. You are under the radar. You are operating to a large extent outside the bureaucracy. Appreciate it." Whereas with the men who are *sannyasis* there is always somebody looking over your shoulder, saying, "Where are you going? What are you doing?" Women who are living like *sannyasis* don't have that. Women are freer, and I would like that to stay under the radar and not really be brought to people's attention. Let it not be noticed that there are a bunch of renounced women not being regulated that way. People don't generally recognise who and what they are and what they are doing. They are just not noticed by the bureaucracy.

In this way it makes it possible for such a woman to develop her spirituality, I would say, more like a traditional *sannyasi* who is not under some institutional bureaucracy. She can live a life that is much more like a traditional *sannyasi* than the men can do in ISKCON. They can do it, too, but it is much easier for a woman. This also allows women to define their own status. It allows them to look at *shastra* and make sure that it is defined according to tradition, rather than having some outside person define it according to institutional rules.

There is a disadvantage, too. The disadvantage is lack of recognition and therefore not being given the same facility. But this is such a minor difference. Yet the disadvantage is there. I mean if a male *sannyasi* comes, there is a certain feeling in a community that everyone has to come along, that a spiritually advanced person is going to be speaking. When a woman who is living as a *sannyasi* comes, on the other hand, there is not that same social pressure and social attitude. But I don't think that this is really what matters, anyway. In another sense this is an advantage for women as well because they are not caught up in that social pressure and prestige, which can become just another designation as well as a source of pride.

There are places where I go in the world and am not allowed to speak from the *vyasasana* because I am a woman. It's absurd, and in some places it is very painful and very difficult. But generally this is not the case. The women who are most disturbed by it are the women who spend most of their time in those places. There are women who are living like *sannyasis*

women, although there is no sanction in the Vedic literature for a woman's accepting *sannyasa*." (*Srimad Bhagavatam* 3.24.40 Purport) and who are really disturbed by the difference between the male and female renounced orders. They are usually the ones living in places where women are really ill-treated.

But I am fairly sure that ISKCON will never formally give *sannyasa* to women because Prabhupada was opposed to it. However, I would like to see ISKCON have some sort of recognition for renounced women. In the *Srimad Bhagavatam* renounced women are said to be in the *vanaprastha ashrama*, and there are different kinds of *vanaprastha*. Most *vanaprastha* women were married and had children, and became older and then became renounced. Some *vanaprastha* women never married. We do have women in our Vaishnava tradition who are called Goswaminis, like Gangamati Goswamini.[9] But I don't expect that to happen in ISKCON at all.

As far as women gurus are concerned, I certainly hope that happens. The lack of women I see is in the broader category of understanding guru, as there are conceptions of guru that are not following guru, *sadhu* and *shastra*, and that I see as the main threat to ISKCON's continuation as a spiritual movement. Whether or not we understand the issue of guru-hood, I see women as part of that picture.

When I speak at events, both men and women will frequently say that they like seeing a senior preacher who is a woman, that they like seeing that you don't have to be a man in that role. I also hear a lot that they like to hear preaching from a female perspective and that it is different, that it does give a different viewpoint. One reason that it is a different perspective is because most of the male *sannyasi*s were never married. I heard that we have just approved or initiated the first *sannyasi* in ISKCON who actually went through a normal marriage and family life, with an occupation and children. With our other *sannyasi*s either they were married and had children for a very brief period of time and then went to live in an ashram, or they were married for some time and never had any children. So I think I bring a different perspective just from that point of view. And people will say that they are so glad to hear a female preacher. That is one of the reasons I keep doing it. I get so much positive feedback that I have not wanted to give it up.

9   Gangmata Goswamini Gangamata (1601-1721) was originally named Saci, and was daughter of the Bengali king Naresh Narayana. According to tradition, she was learned and saintly and joined the Gaudiya Vaishnava line, becoming a disciple of Hari Das Pandit Goswami. She never married but instead became absorbed in a life of austerity. She lived as a renunciate teacher in Vrindavan and also in Jaganath Puri. Today branches of the Math she established are found in Puri and in Cuttack in the Indian state of Orissa.

Concluding Thoughts and Reflections

One point that needs to keep on being emphasised is that ISKCON is not a monolithic organisation. It is vastly varied sociologically speaking, being different in different parts of the world and sometimes even in different parts of the same country. I have not noticed any difference in terms of ISKCON's core teachings: chant Hare Krishna; Krishna is God; there is a spiritual goal; we are not this body; there is karma and there is reincarnation. These teachings are found everywhere in ISKCON. Also, the basic rituals are essentially the same. There is some variation to be found but it is very slight. However, from a sociological perspective ISKCON is vastly different in different places indeed, even though it is the same organisation.

There are some areas and some personalities with great influence in all of this diversity. I would say that what Radhanath Swami has done has really affected ISKCON globally. He is one of the few people who have a very strong global influence. Devamrita Swami has also had a significant global influence, but not as strong as that of Radhanath Swami.[10] Devamrita Swami's yoga programme has had a huge impact. I would point out that whatever happens in Vrindavan and Maypaur affects the world of ISKCON too, because so many devotees go there and then later return to their different places or centres. Whatever standards are being set in Vrindavan and Mayapur have a big effect in this way.

Devotees who are producing books further have a major influence on ISKCON today. Here I would say that Mahanidhi Swami has a big effect on ISKCON, even though he just sits in a little place at Radha-kund in Vrindavan. He does not travel much and it is very hard to see him. But his effect on ISKCON is absolutely huge. Others who have been highly influential form a kind of a group, though they don't all work together all of the time. They include Sacinandana Swami, Bhurijana Das, Mahatma Das, Braja Bihari Dasa, and Janmashtami Dasa.[11] These are the figures

---

10 Devamrita Swami was born in 1950 in New York City and studied at Yale University. He became a *sannyasi* in ISKCON in 1982 and in 2002 accepted the post of initiating spiritual master. Currently, he is based in Australia and in New Zealand, and frequently travels to India on preaching missions. ISKCON guru and *sannyasi* Radhanath Swami is based largely at the centre he heads in Mumbai, India, and he is widely regarded by Hare Krishna devotees throughout the world as being the most inspirational spiritual leader in ISKCON today.

11 Sacinandana Swami is an ISKCON guru and *sannyasi* who has translated the *Bhagavad Gita* into German and who has also written a number of devotional texts. He has conducted classes at the Vaishnava Institute for Higher Education in Vrindavan, India and has taught classes at Bhaktivedanta College in Radhadesh, Belgium. He also serves as the Spiritual Director of the Veda Academy, an

who have established the *japa* retreats, *kirtan* retreats and *kirtan* week-ends. The *shastric* classes which started in Vrindavan have equally had a huge effect on ISKCON internationally, and this has had an impact on ISKCON wherever you go in the world. Furthermore, I would say that Kurma Dasa,[12] who introduced international cooking, has had a huge effect on ISKCON. Yet another highly influential individual in ISKCON is Lokanatha Swami because of his *padayatra* (walking pilgrimage); and there have been many of these *padayatra*s all over the world because of him. What he did with the Centennial event permanently transformed ISKCON.[13]

So there are certain international trends that are being promoted by certain individuals or by some groups of individuals, such as those already mentioned. Some of them do this by travelling, like Sacinandana Swami.

internationally recognized university of Vedic sciences, arts, and philosophy active in eight different countries. Bhurijana Das, an early disciple of Prabhupada, opened ISKCON's first Hong Kong centre in 1970. Since 1977 he has taught both in New York and in Vrindavan. In Vrindavan in 1987 he began the Vaishnava Institute for Higher Education, where he has taught courses in teaching, writing, and the principal books of Prabhupada. Mahatma Das is well known in ISKCON for his recorded music and for his seminars. He is the founder of Touchstone Training, a company that teaches the practices of devotional service through interactive seminars and workshops. He is also a facilitator in Bhagavat Life, producers of live and online workshops, and he is a key organiser of *japa* retreats. He resides in Alachua, Florida. Braja Bihari Dasa is Director of ISKCON Resolve, a service set up by the GBC in 2002 to provide help and advice to devotees suffering from a variety of social or interrelational problems within the global ISKCON community. Janmashtami Dasa started the Mayapur Institute for Higher Education, which offers courses in *shastra* as well as other practical courses for devotees at ISKCON's world headquarters in West Bengal. He is one of the pioneers of adult education and his role in all this work is similar overall to the work of Bhurijana Das already mentioned above.

12 Kurma Dasa has held the post of head chef for many years at Melbourne's popular Gopal's Restaurant. He is the author of a number of highly acclaimed cookery books: Dasa, Kurma (1990) *Great Vegetarian Dishes*. Los Angeles: Bhaktivedanta Book Trust; Dasa, Kurma (1998) *Cooking with Kurma*. Botany: Chakra; Dasa, Kurma (2000) *Quick Vegetarian Dishes*. Botany: Chakra; Dasa, Kurma (2002) *Vegetarian World Food*. Botany: Chakra. Kurma Dasa has also taught his special brand of eclectic gourmet vegetarian cuisine throughout Australia and around the world. He has hosted three internationally broadcast television cooking series seen in over 46 different countries. Currently, he is working on more cookbooks and is presenting gourmet vegetarian cooking master classes overseas and throughout Australia, as well as writing columns for a variety of magazines.

13 1996 was Prabhupada's centennial year (i.e., 100 years after his birth). During that year there was a huge increase in festival activities. Lokanatha Swami's *padayatra* event, which involves a walking procession between temples and places of pilgrimage, became popular at this time and has remained popular in subsequent years. Indian-born Lokanatha Swami himself is an ISKCON guru and is based mostly in the Indian state of Maharashtra.

Others inform or help shape ISKCON by remaining in one place. Aindra Dasa,[14] for example, did that. And one point in all of this that should be kept in mind is that almost all of these figures I have mentioned have tended to operate somewhat outside the bureaucracy of ISKCON; that is, they have had some independence from the tight bureaucracy. They may have been members of the bureaucracy itself but in their own spheres they have been able to operate somewhat autonomously.

Returning to the important point again about ISKCON not being monolithic, we, therefore, have to be wary of arguments from sociologists who take what they see in certain centres in one country and then generalise from them to ISKCON as a whole or as an international organisation. This is not the case at all. It is not accurate.

---

14 Aindra Dasa (1953–2010) is of American origin and was a renunciate. He was a talented and inspiring musician and singer. In 1977 he moved to ISKCON Balaram Temple in Vrindavan, India, where he was based for the rest of his life. There he oversaw the 24-Hour *kirtan* programme, which ensured that the Hare Krishna mantra was sung in the temple room almost continuously.

9. Final Remarks: The Legacy Of A. C. Bhaktivedanta Swami Prabhupada

By Dr Michael J. Gressett

In February 1974 I first visited a Krishna temple and witnessed a young devotee rapidly ascending a staircase carrying a fragrant, covered tray, exclaiming, "Lord's plates! Lord's plates!"[1] Along with their clothing of *dhotis* and *saris*, and every other word in Sanskrit, it was as if I had been transported to medieval India. The charm of it all was that India had come to the West and in two dimensions: as a quaint, foreign culture and as a religious specialist's approach to that culture. But from the beginning of Prabhupada's efforts in the West, most people who were attracted to his teachings did not become religious specialists. Prabhupada's achievement stands because first, second and third generations of devotees all over the world continue to believe in God as a beautiful blue person, a Lord who hungers for offerings of love. Because the scene I witnessed was the creation of a single charismatic individual, nearly 40 years later it seems appropriate to wonder what he would think of his legacy, an attempt to inculcate what he called "the cult of Chaitanya." This was before the term was misappropriated by antagonistic religionists and a sensationalist press. But the sense of something unusual remains, or as cognitive science researcher Kimmo Ketola points out, because the Krishna movement "has managed to avert tedium."[2] This is extraordinary; for in the normal course of events "when a religion has become itself an orthodoxy, its day of inwardness is over: the spring is dry; the faithful live at secondhand exclusively and stone the prophets in their turn..."[3]

I live in North Florida, which has the largest community of Krishna devotees in the Western hemisphere. It is a truly international community, and I have not seen any lessening of enthusiasm, even though

---

1   In Hinduism, iconic deities are worshiped as the residing Lord of a temple or as an honoured guest in one's home, and served food and other items in rituals.

2   Ketola, Kimmo (2008) *The Founder of the Hare Krishnas as Seen by Devotees: A Cognitive Study of Religious Charisma.* Boston: Brill, p. 82.

3   James, William (2002) *The Varieties of Religious Experience: A Study in Human Nature, Being the Gifford Lectures on Natural Religion Delivered at Edinburgh in 1901-1902.* New York: The Modern Library, p. 369.

Prabhupada's teachings had already been orthodoxy before he arrived in America. The founder remains as both a priestly and a prophetical figure of the highest reputation among his followers, but his teachings are now interpreted—in one way or another—by secondary, intuitive means for the everyday practice of lived religion.[4] Except for the most general ideas—that Krishna is the supreme spiritual reality and can be attained by the practice of devotion, for instance—there was never a single understanding of Prabhupada's primary teachings, and that is so much more the case today.

I see complexity as a pivotal issue for understanding the spread of Chaitanya's religion because Prabhupada was dedicated to the orthodox and orthoprax propagation of his *sampradaya*, or formal school, not the spread of a generalised devotion to Krishna. The founder once quipped, "I have one disease. I only think big."[5] Consequently, he compared his agenda for his disciples—the people who did not return to their homes after the Sunday feast—to a quick elevator trip to the spiritual world, as compared to taking the stairs. Focusing on the "vertical" dimension of consciousness elevation spirituality, Prabhupada did take the time to inform his disciples of the four valid concerns of human life—religion, acquisition of the necessities of life, fulfilment of desires, and liberation from the cycle of birth and death—but he only encouraged concentration on the first and last of these concerns. Furthermore, his teaching in a sense went beyond even liberation, as Chaitanya confessed: "I only want your devotional service, birth after birth."[6] Prabhupada must have known that the vast entity we call Hinduism had hitched a ride to the West along with his *sampradaya*, and it would be only a matter of time before people realised that the ethos of the *Mahabharata*, for instance, is different from the *Srimad Bhagavatam*. There is even less place for

---

4 According to Max Weber, a prophet tends to confront the religious establishment of his or her society, and a priest tends to represent it. Because Prabhupada embodied a foreign religious culture in the West, his career falls within both categories. For a detailed discussion of Weber's ideas about religious charisma involving these terms, see Ketola, Kimmo (2008) *The Founder of the Hare Krishnas as Seen by Devotees: A Cognitive Study of Religious Charisma*. Boston: Brill.

5 Friends of the BBT (2007) Vijaya Dasa, December. friendsofthebbt.org/newsletter/Dec07.html.

6 Chaitanya is considered to be Krishna himself in the role of a devotee, who left eight instructions in Sanskrit, the *Siksastaka*. The example he sets in the fourth instruction, "O almighty Lord, I have no desire to accumulate wealth, nor do I desire beautiful women, nor do I want any number of followers," I only want Your causeless devotional service birth after birth," should dispel any doubt that his tradition is ascetic at its core. See Svami, Acyutananda (1974) *Songs of the Vaishnava Ācāryas*. Los Angeles: Bhaktivedanta Book Trust, p. 25.

worldliness in the *Caitanya Caritamrta*. But, as most Hindus will affirm, you could be a devotee of Krishna and yet maintain a legitimate interest in the enjoyment of material things. Indeed, most people in the Vedic age did not follow Prabhupada's ascetic view of marriage, and even taking a drink did not devalue a person. The heroes of the *Mahabharata* revere ascetics, but they don't live like them. Although the Vedic world of the *Mahabharata* is quite different from our modern world, even so, the spiritual abilities of the average modern person are closer to that world than they are to Chaitanya's utter lack of interest in ordinary things. More than one devotee has commented that Prabhupada was so strict because he knew that his charming but rigorous teachings would be chipped away, bit by bit.

Understandably, in this volume Steven Rosen has lamented the disappearance of ascetic standards in the second generation of Krishna devotees; for the founder's preference was clear. But Prabhupada was expert at settling for half a loaf. At first he requested that his disciples recite 64 rounds of the Hare Krishna mantra, but they haggled and finally agreed on 16. Ethnic Hindus, having lived with a guru culture for thousands of years, are perhaps more likely to take spiritual teachings in their stride; for Krishna has explained that spiritual perfection is accomplished after many births.[7] Hindus throughout the world also consistently set the example for a "horizontal" dimension of spiritual life, in which family life is prominent. It should be remembered that Chaitanya as well as Prabhupada were raised in a social environment of creative tension between the values of Narada and Daksha, Vedic proponents of transcendence and this-worldly interests, respectively.[8] Saints tend to appear in a social atmosphere of established, family-oriented religion. If devotees follow Daksha as well as Narada, it seems that Prabhupada is still getting his half a loaf.

As for the foreign element, we can look to the global village that our planet has become and ask if cultural practices are now deliberate choices, or remain only memes, cultural analogues to genes that self-replicate without conscious effort. John Esposito, referencing Peter Berger, has

---

7   Prabhupada, A. C. Bhaktivedanta Swami (1972) *Bhagavad Gita As It Is*. New York: The Macmillan Company. Chapter 7, Verse 19: "After many births and deaths, he who is actually in knowledge surrenders unto Me, knowing Me to be the cause of all causes and all that is. Such a great soul is very rare."

8   Prabhupada made a special point of contrasting the lifestyles and values of sage Narada, who lived like an ascetic, with Daksha, a married householder who considered material enjoyment to be a valid goal of life. See Canto Six, Chapter Five, Narada Muni Cursed By Prajapati Daksa in Prabhupada, A. C. Bhaktivedanta Swami (1975) *Srimad Bhagavatam*. Los Angeles: Bhaktivedanta Book Trust.

remarked that everyone in modernity is a religious heretic—someone who simply chooses.[9] This development has been and remains favourable for Prabhupada's mission because it means opportunity for an alternative view. However, any consideration of culture means that we need more research on Krishna devotion in various world locations. Fascination with charisma will be found in any devotee community, but the individualism that informs the American religious experience, for instance, may not pertain to Russia, which has developed its Krishna Consciousness almost exclusively without American influence.

Wherever this tradition goes, transplantation is perhaps an inappropriate metaphor for its syncretistic growth. In Alachua, Florida, where the New Raman Reti community is now in its fourth decade, devotees have been consulted by the pagan community about how to worship a variety of Hindu deities. A gay man from this community recently gave his partner *Bhagavad Gita As It Is* for a Valentine's Day present. A friend of mine, an ethnic Hindu in England, reveres Prabhupada as well as Swami Vivekananda, whom Prabhupada sharply disagreed with. A devotee from Cuba somehow finds Krishna Consciousness compatible with the doctrines of Karl Marx. I have seen Krishna Consciousness mixed with love of Jesus, and there are people known to me in California who go to their synagogue on Saturday and the Krishna temple on Sunday. I witnessed an instance of Kali possession facilitated by Krishna devotees as a personal growth process in Alachua. Some of Prabhupada's disciples are upset by these kinds of development. But as a counterpoint, more than one second-generation devotee have expressed the view to me in interviews that their parents did not understand Prabhupada's teachings, and they expect the movement will improve when their parents' generation passes away.[10] Perhaps this assessment is not so grim, as it was Prabhupada who remarked that it would require three generations to produce pure devotees. Only time will tell if these devotees will agree with the founder on every detail. It could be argued that the founder provided for further new initiatives when he requested his disciples to put his teachings into their own words; for it is unlikely that such translation across cultural

9   Esposito, John; Darrel J Fashing; Todd Lewis (2009) *Religions of Asia Today*. Oxford: Oxford University Press, p. 32.

10   In 2006-2009, I conducted interviews with Americans and ethnic Hindus in the Alachua area, including devotees, friends of devotees, and neighbours, ranging from temple administrators to people who rarely or never visited the local Krishna temple, and conversed with them by email and telephone, on matters pertaining to their opinions and perceptions of the Krishna movement and its place in American society.

boundaries would lack innovation. Yet others are still inclined to quote Prabhupada's assertion that his books would be law for 10,000 years.[11]

Organised religion has suffered a crisis in credibility almost everywhere, so in interviews carried out for my own PhD dissertation, I was not surprised when I did not discover a single second-generation devotee who—much like their parents—gave any importance to ISKCON's Governing Body Commission (GBC) as an institutional body. Yet the aversion to institutions is not uniform, and women in particular have made significant progress in ISKCON. But, ironically, although the Alachua temple has had female presidents for some 15 years, few women lecture there. Many have insisted it was because they did not want to, while others feel unwelcome. Such issues are illuminated by varying research perspectives, yet consensus on details eludes academic and devotee scholars alike. The following scenario convinced me that rich opportunities for interpretation abound. As I was doing research for my PhD dissertation, I witnessed a group of first-generation men and women in the *prasada* (sacred food) line at the Sunday programme discussing the view that women should not be leaders, when the daughter of a GBC representative turned and silenced them with a glare.

Although women do not typically administrate or perform temple rituals in India as they do throughout the Western world, the temple scene in the West now resembles Indian temples because the devotee communities use the temple for their own purposes, whereas in the past these communities existed to serve the temple and its preaching mission. Edith Best and other contributors in this volume have commented that Western temples now stand empty most of the time, but this seems quite natural. Like their Hindu brethren, I myself have observed that when visiting a temple, most Western devotees just want to see the deities, perform *kirtana* and take *prasadam*. It is not that they have anything against the temple, but they do have jobs. I have not noticed that home *puja* has often replaced temple worship, although household cultivation of the sacred tulasi integral to Krishna devotion has become common—like in India—even without the strict practices that some devotees have imagined as a requirement for cultivating this plant.[12] If Indians are

---

11 Prabhupada saw himself as a messenger, not a creator, of spiritual doctrines and standards, and predicted that his books would be seen as authoritative "law books" for 10,000 years. See Ekkehard Lorenz (2003) Who Needs Authentic Books? Chakra website, January 31. www.chakra.org/discussions/BMJan31_03.html.

12 Tulasi (*ocimum sanctum*) is a small shrub or plant with medicinal properties, but it is only used for worship by Krishna devotees, who consider it to be a goddess descended to Earth out of compassion for "conditioned souls."

becoming more involved in ISKCON temples, would not this please the founder? Recently I was startled by what seemed to be the reincarnation of Prabhupada's *diksha* guru Bhaktisiddhanta Sarasvati Thakura—the likeness was so strong, especially with his Gaudiya Vaishnava *tilaka* and wire-rim glasses—performing *seva* or service in the temple kitchen. Of course, he was an engineer.

Many devotees are comfortable with medieval ideas about the natural world even as they earn academic degrees in science. And to be realistic about our modern or postmodern world, just as there are educated Christians who still believe in the Resurrection, we must acknowledge that modernists do not own modernity. Nor have I noticed any institutional schisms in ISKCON, so far, based on a traditionalist-modernist split, as divisions have more or less been confined to succession issues. This may or may not be problematic for a religious institution, but for any religious expression it broadens market share because the sectarian impulse—as sociologist of religion Rodney Stark uses the concept—offers more religious market niches.[13] For Stark, a church is an established religion with low tension and influence in society, a sect breaks away from a church on the issue of reform, and a cult is an entirely new religious expression, homegrown, or imported. Using the term cult non-pejoratively, Prabhupada's legacy, although a church in India, constitutes a cult movement outside of India because the founder meant it to become a church, even though it has already produced sects.

Regardless of numerous real scandals as well as misrepresentation by (mostly) non-academic commentators, the Hare Krishna movement's reputation has actually improved over the years through mainstream public relations practices. One of the most fascinating manifestations of Prabhupada's legacy can be found in Moscow, where the devotees sponsor a billboard of the cover of *Bhagavad Gita As It Is* in the metro system. Millions of Russians have thus now seen the iconic image of Krishna on a battlefield, and some have come to agree with Henry David Thoreau that in ancient times the god had contributed to world literature a "stupendous and cosmogonal philosophy."[14] When a new religious movement becomes a household name in this way, it is well on its way to becoming a church. 60,000 pilgrims attending a festival at Bhaktivedanta Manor near Watford would qualify Prabhupada's legacy in the UK as a church by almost anyone's standard. In Mayapur, India, the birthplace of Chaitanya,

---

13 See Stark, Rodney (1979). Of Churches, Sects, and Cults: Preliminary Concepts for a Theory of Religious Movements in *Journal for the Scientific Study of Religion* 18 (2).

14 See Thoreau, Henry David (1906) *Walden or Life In The Woods*. Boston and New York: Houghton, Mifflin Company, p. 328.

the Temple of the Vedic Planetarium currently under construction has captured the imagination of the Hindu world, and Bhaktivinoda's prediction that an international devotee community would be established on this site has already come to pass.

The movement, however, is expanding in other locations with little reference to the categories of new religious movement and church, where inculcation of theology and attention to precise social science categories would be almost beside the point. In the war-torn Democratic Republic of Congo, for example, a second-generation devotee from America is organising a successful rural community around Prabhupada's vision of a self-sufficient Vedic village, essentially the same as Gandhi's vision. The workers are free to emulate the director's religious example or continue with their animist, Christian, or Islamic heritage. The main point of this village is to build spiritual values, literally, from the ground up. "Within ten miles nobody should remain hungry," Prabhupada once said, and so the two main projects here are agriculture and building construction.[15] Many devotees have thus concluded that cultivating Krishna Consciousness anywhere in the world fulfils both their personal *dharma* and, somehow, assists Chaitanya's vow that his name would be heard in every town and village, which was exactly what Prabhupada wanted.

In closing, this book represents a critical mass, the culmination of over 40 years of scholarship; and the near-consensus of its contributors on many important issues deepens understanding of ISKCON devotees and their concerns as they struggle to make their religion a church. When an entire religious culture is brought out of its native land singlehandedly and established internationally by a handful of callow novices, it is little wonder that the scholarly world remains fascinated with the generations who follow. That is Prabhupada's legacy, and "the story of Prabhupada's sacrificial life," as Stillson Judah put it, convinces me that, regardless of the fulfilment of his *sampradaya* emphasis, he would be satisfied that the spirit of his "lawbooks," if not their letter, has been firmly established.[16]

Bibliography

Esposito, John; Darrel J Fashing; Todd Lewis (2009) *Religions of Asia Today*. Oxford: Oxford University Press, p. 32.

---

15 Folio: Bhaktivedanta *VedaBase* 2003.1 [Shadow] (1977) Conversation and instruction on new movie, Allahabad, 770113rc.all.

16 See Stillson Judah in Gosvami, Satsvarupa Dasa (1981) *Srila Prabhupada-lilamrta Volume 3: Only He Could Lead Them.* Los Angeles: Bhaktivedanta Book Trust, p. viii.

Folio: Bhaktivedanta *VedaBase* 2003.1 [Shadow] (1977) Conversation and instruction on new movie, Allahabad, 770113rc.all.

Friends of the BBT (2007) Vijaya Dasa friendsofthebbt.org/newsletter/Dec07.html.

Gosvami, Satsvarupa Dasa (1981) *Srila Prabhupada-lilamrta Volume 3: Only He Could Lead Them.* Los Angeles: Bhaktivedanta Book Trust.

Gressett, Michael (2009) PhD Dissertation. *From Krishna Cult to American Church: The Dialectical Quest for Spiritual Dwelling in the Modern Krishna Movement in the West.* University of Florida etd.fcla.edu/UF/UFE0024749/gressett_m.pdf.

James, William (2002) *The Varieties of Religious Experience: A Study in Human Nature, Being the Gifford Lectures on Natural Religion Delivered at Edinburgh in 1901-190.* New York: The Modern Library.

Ketola, Kimmo (2008) *The Founder of the Hare Krishnas as Seen by Devotees: A Cognitive Study of Religious Charisma.* Boston: Brill.

(2002) PhD Dissertation. An Indian Guru and his Western Disciples: Representation and Communication of Charisma in the Hare Krishna Movement. University of Helsinki ethesis.helsinki.fi/julkaisut/hum/uskon/vk/ketola/anindian.pdf.

Lorenz, Ekkehard (2003) *Who Needs Authentic Books?* Chakra website, January 31. www.chakra.org/discussions/BMJan31_03.html.

Prabhupada, A. C. Bhaktivedanta Swami (1972) *Bhagavad Gita As It Is.* New York: The Macmillan Company.

(1972) *Srimad Bhagavatam.* Los Angeles: Bhaktivedanta Book Trust.

(1989) *Sri Caitanya Caritamrta.* Los Angeles: Bhaktivedanta Book Trust.

Stark, Rodney (1979) Of Churches, Sects, and Cults: Preliminary Concepts for a Theory of Religious Movements. *Journal for the Scientific Study of Religion* 18 (2).

Svami, Acyutananda (1974) *Songs of the Vaisnava Acaryas.* Los Angeles: Bhaktivedanta Book Trust.

Thoreau, Henry David (1906) *Walden or Life in the Woods*. Boston and New York: Houghton, Mifflin Company.

van Buitenen, J.A.B. (1973) tr., *The Mahabharata*. London and Chicago: University of Chicago Press.

Glossary of Sanskrit and Other Key Terms

acharya   elevated spiritual master who teaches by his own
                             example

arati   rite of worship typically involving the clockwise cir-
                             cling of a ritual object (e.g. lamp, incense stick, conch
                             shell) before the image of a deity *ashram* monastic
                             institution or community; stage of life of which there
                             are four orders: celibate student life (*brahmacharya*),
                             householder life (*grihastha*), retired life (*vanaprastha*),
                             and renounced life (*sannyasa*).

Bhagavad Gita   literally, "Song of the Divine One"; a major episode
                             in the great epic Sanskrit work *Mahabharata* and a
                             text in which Krishna as the Supreme Personality of
                             Godhead appears in order to give instruction to the
                             warrior Arjuna

Bhagavata Purana   Sanskrit text celebrating the life of Krishna, His
                             various incarnations and devotees (cf. *Srimad
                             Bhagavatam*)

bhajan   hymn; devotional song

bhakta/bhaktin   male/female devotee

bhakti   loving devotion to Godhead

Bhaktivedanta Narayana
Mahraja   younger Bengali contemporary and godbrother of
                             Bhaktivedanta Swami Prabhupada Bhaktivedanta
                             Swami

Prabhupada   founder of ISKCON, the Hare Krishna movement

vaidhi-bhakti-sadhana   standard devotional service; study and meditation;
                             the four regulative principles: (1) to abstain from all
                             meat, fish or eggs; (2) to avoid all forms of intoxication
                             (including tea, coffee and tobacco); (3) to abstain from
                             gambling; and (4) to avoid sex except for the purpose
                             of procreation within marriage

bhakti-yoga   the path or way of devotion

brahmachari(n)	celibate student/monk (nun)
brahmana	ritual technician or priest (cf. *pujari*)
Chaitanya Mahaprabhu	15th-16th century Bengali ecstatic considered in ISKCON to be non-different from Krishna and Radha combined
dalit	low caste person; untouchable
dharma	virtue, morality, order, righteousness, religion; socio-religious duty
dhoti	loin cloth worn by men
diksha	initiation
Gaudiya Vaishnavism	the tradition of Vaishnavism inaugurated by Chaitanya; known also as Chaitanya Vaishnavism
GBC	Governing Body Commission; ISKCON's ruling power base, possessing ultimate authority and formed by the founder of ISKCON in July 1970
*grihastha*a	married man or woman; householder life
gurukuli	one who is or who has studied in a *gurukula*, a religious school (of ISKCON)
Hari Nama	chanting the Hare Krishna mantra in public locations (cf. *kirtana, sankirtana*)
IRM	ISKCON Reform/Revival Movement
ISKCON	International Society for Krishna Consciousness; the Hare Krishna movement
japa	mantra or sacred verse uttered repetitively
kirtana	devotional chanting of mantras (cf. *sankirtana*)
Krishna	the Supreme Personality of Godhead in Gaudiya Vaishnavism of which ISKCON is a branch
mahamantra	the Hare Krishna mantra: *Hare Krishna, Hare Krishna, Krishna Krishna, Hare Hare/ Hare Rama, Hare Rama, Rama Rama, Hare Hare.*
mataji	honorific term, meaning "respected mother"; term of respect used to address female devotees
mayavadin	an adherent of *mayavada* philosophy; one who conceives of "God" or the Absolute in impersonal terms
murti	image of a deity

mundan	ritual tonsure; head shaving ceremony for young boys
nama hatta	house groups; system of organised gatherings that take place in the homes of devotees for purposes of worship and scripture study
Pandava Sena	organisation of youth or young people in ISKCON
parampara	disciplic succession; lineage of spiritual masters or gurus (cf. *sampradaya*)
prasadam	sanctified food; sacred remains of food offered to Lord Krishna and later distributed to devotees and to the wider public
puja	worship
pujari	priest; one who carries out ceremonial acts, especially the congregational rite of worship
ritvik	the guru's representative viewed in ISKCON as one who has been given authority to act on behalf of the guru for the purpose of initiation while the guru is still living
sadhana	ritual method or spiritual practice
sadhu	world renouncer; mendicant; holy man (cf. *sannyasi*)
sampradaya	established doctrine transmitted from one guru or teacher to another; lineage of gurus
sankirtana	congregational chanting of mantras; chanting the names of God in public locations
sannyasa	renunciation, renounced life
sannyasi	renouncer; one who has renounced all worldly ties and duties
seva	service; task or duty performed as an act of devotion to god
shastra	scripture
Srimad Bhagavatam	Bhaktivedanta Swami Prabhupada's English translation of, and commentary on, the *Bhagavata Purana*
tapas	austerity, performed as an expression of devotion
tirtha	ritual bathing place; place of pilgrimage usually on the banks of sacred rivers
vanaprastha	retired life

varnashrama/
varnasharamadharmas   ocio-religious organisation in ancient India com-
                          prised of four categories of person, viz., priest/
                          teacher (*brahmana*), warrior/leader/administrator
                          (*kshatriya*), farmer/merchant (*vaishya*), and servant/
                          labourer (*shudra*)

vyasasana   seat of guru

Notes on Contributors

Edith Best (Urmila Devi Dasi) became an initiated disciple of A. C. Bhaktivedanta Swami Prabhupada in 1973, and she has an EdD and MSA from the University of North Carolina at Chapel Hill. She is Professor of Sociology and ISKCON History at Bhaktivedanta College in Radhadesh, Belgium and is an associate editor of *Back to Godhead, the Magazine of the Hare Krishna Movement*. She is the author of numerous articles on education and spiritual life, including a book on teaching and school management: *Vaikuntha Children, a Complete Classroom Guidebook for K-12*, (North Carolina: ISKCON Education of North Carolina, Inc., 1992; 2nd Edition, North Carolina: Padma Inc., 2010). She has also written and produced an 83 book set to teach elementary school children how to read English: *Dr. Best Learn to Read* (London: Mantralingua, 2010). She taught primary school children for 27 years, 18 of which she was also principal of elementary and secondary schools in ISKCON. For 10 years she was a member of ISKCON's International Board of Education and for seven years was Vice-Chairman of the North American Board. She continues to develop and teach local, national, and international seminars for trainers, educators, and managers, and she is a member of the Sastric Advisory Council to the Governing Body Commission of the International Society for Krishna Consciousness.

Richard J. Cole (Radha Mohan Das) has a BA in Media and Performance from the University of Salford. He is Secretary of ISKCON's Communications Department at Bhaktivedanta Manor, where he is responsible for work with the media, publications, political VIPs and interfaith groups. He regularly gives presentations on Krishna Consciousness but specialises in writing and performing dramas based on India's Vedic scriptures. He was a researcher for the book by Joshua Greene, *Here Comes the Sun: The Spiritual and Musical Journey of George Harrison* (New York: Wiley, 2006); helped in the publication of a number of children's books, and in collaboration with Graham Dwyer he has contributed to and edited a collection of essays on the Hare Krishna movement: Dwyer, Graham and Richard J. Cole. (Eds.) *The Hare Krishna Movement: Forty Years of Chant and Change* (London and New York: IB Tauris, 2007).

Graham Dwyer has a BA in Religious Studies and Sociology from the University of Lancaster, received his MSt and DPhil in Social Anthropology from the University of Oxford and is currently Honorary Research Fellow at the Centre for Theology and Religious Studies, University of Winchester. He has carried out research on vernacular Hinduism in Rajasthan, concentrating on spirit possession and exorcism, and has authored both articles and a monograph on the topic: *The Divine and the Demonic: Supernatural Affliction and its Treatment in North India* (London and New York: RoutledgeCurzon, 2003). His interest in the International Society for Krishna Consciousness (ISKCON) became the major focus of Dwyer's research in 2002. He has written a number of scholarly articles and essays on ISKCON as well as co-edited a book on the Krishna Consciousness movement: Dwyer, Graham and Richard J. Cole. (Eds.) *The Hare Krishna Movement: Forty Years of Chant and Change* (London and New York: IB Tauris, 2007). He has also been research consultant, co-script writer and assistant director on a film about ISKCON directed by Finnish documentary filmmaker Jouko Aaltonen, *Leap*, released in 2012 (leapthefilm.com).

Joshua M. Greene is Adjunct Professor of Religious Studies at Hofstra University and Fordham Lincoln Center. His books on Holocaust history include *Witness: Voices from the Holocaust* (New York: Simon and Schuster, 2000) and *Justice at Dachau* (New York: Random House, 2003). He produces documentary films for PBS (America's Public Broadcasting System), most recently *Hitler's Courts: Betrayal of the Rule of Law in Nazi Germany* (2007). His yoga-related works include *Gita Wisdom: An Introduction to India's Essential Yoga Text* (California: Mandala, 2008), *Here Comes the Sun: The Spiritual and Musical Journey of George Harrison* (New York: John Wiley and Sons, 2006), and the documentary *Living Yoga* (2008), which traces the rise of yoga culture in America. Since 2005 he has taught weekly *Bhagavad Gita* classes at Jivamukti Yoga School in New York.

Michael J. Gressett has a BA in Religious Studies from the University of California at Berkeley, as well as an MA and a PhD specialising in Asian religions and new religious movements from the University of Florida. His PhD dissertation, *From Krishna Cult to American Church: The Dialectical Quest for Spiritual Dwelling in the Modern Krishna Movement in the West*, is an expression of his interest in the Hare Krishna movement both as an academic and as a devotee since 1974, when he was initiated by A. C. Bhaktivedanta Swami Prabhupada. He has published reviews and encyclopedia articles about the movement and teaches Philosophy and Religion at Florida Gateway College. His current research and writing projects are directed at critiquing established scholarship on the movement and religion in general, as well as have a focus on the influence of religion in human potential seminars.

Anna S. King is Reader in Theology and Religious Studies, Faculty of Humanities and Social Sciences, University of Winchester. Her research and teaching interests include South Asian religious traditions and subcontinental and global Islam. Anna trained as a social anthropologist at the Institute of Social and Cultural Anthropology in Oxford. Her publications include *The Intimate Other: Love Divine in Indic Religions* edited with John Brockington (New Delhi: Orient Longman, 2005) and *Indian Religions: Renaissance and Renewal* (London: Equinox, 2006), as well as scholarly articles in, for example, *The Persistent Challenge: Religion, Truth, and Scholarship, Essays in Honour of Klaus Klostermaier* (Eds. I. Bocken, W. Dupre, P. van der Velde, Maastricht: Shaker, 2004) and *The Hare Krishna Movement: Forty Years of Chant and Change* (Eds. Graham Dwyer and Richard J. Cole, London and New York: IB Tauris, 2007). She has acted as adviser to a film on ISKCON directed by Jouko Aaltonen, the Finnish ethnographic filmmaker. Her recent papers include Rhetorical Reflections, in *Religion, Terror and Violence: Religious Studies Perspectives*, edited by Bryan Rennie and Philip L. Tite (London: Routledge, 2008); Islam, Women and Violence, in *Feminist Theology* vol. 17, no. 3 (Eds. Lisa Isherwood and Lillalou Hughes); and The Waters of Devotion: Globalising the Ganges, Revalorising Tradition, in *SSEASR Journal* Vol 1V, 2010. Anna is editor of *Religions of South Asia* (RoSA) published twice a year by Equinox (2007-), and convener of the annual Oxford Spalding Symposium on Indian Religions.

Kim Knott is Professor of Religious Studies at the University of Leeds. She is the author of *My Sweet Lord: The Hare Krishna Movement* (Wellingborough: Aquarian Press, 1986) and *Hinduism: A Very Short History* (New York: Oxford University Press, 1998). In addition to her numerous articles and essays on the Krishna Consciousness movement, she has also published widely on issues of religion and identity among religious minorities and on the relationship of religion and ethnicity in Britain.

Julius Lipner is Professor of Hinduism and the Comparative Study of Religion at the University of Cambridge, where he has been teaching for many years. He was born and raised in India, and returns to India on a regular basis to undertake research and to meet friends and relatives. He has lectured and published widely in the UK and abroad in his subject area, and is at present working on the theologies of image-worship in Hindu tradition. His books include *The Face of Truth: A Study of Meaning and Metaphysics in the Vedantic Theology of Ramanuja* (New York: SUNY Press, 1986); *Brahmabandhab Upadhyay: The Life and Thought of a Revolutionary* (Delhi: Oxford University Press, 1999); *Anandamath, or The Sacred Brotherhood* (Delhi: Oxford University Press, 2006); and the second edition of *Hindus: Their Religious Beliefs and Practices* (London and New York: Routledge, 2010). He is a Fellow of the British Academy.

E. Burke Rochford, Jr. is Professor of Religion at Middlebury College in Vermont. Trained as a sociologist he has studied the Hare Krishna movement since 1975. In addition to numerous articles on the movement he has also published *Hare Krishna in America* (New Brunswick: Rutgers University Press, 1985) and *Hare Krishna Transformed* (New York University Press, 2007). His article (with Kendra Bailey), Almost Heaven: Leadership, Decline, and the Transformation of New Vrindaban received the 2006 Thomas Robbins Award for Excellence in the Study of New Religious Movements.

Steven J. Rosen (Satyaraja Dasa) is an initiated disciple of His Divine Grace A.C. Bhaktivedanta Swami Prabhupada. He is also founding editor of the *Journal of Vaishnava Studies* and associate editor of *Back to Godhead*. He has published over 30 books in numerous languages, including the recent *Essential Hinduism* (Lanham: Rowman and Littlefield, 2008); *The Yoga of Kirtan: Conversations on the Sacred Art of Chanting* (New York: FOLK Books, 2008); *Krishna's Other Song: A New Look at the Uddhava Gita* (Westport: Praeger-Greenwood, 2010); and *The Jedi in the Lotus: Star Wars and Hindu Traditions* (London: Arktos, 2010).

Kenneth Valpey was born in 1950 in West Point, New York. After interrupting undergraduate architecture studies at UC Berkeley in 1972, from then until 1995 he participated in missionary and ministerial activity with ISKCON in central Europe. He then resumed academic study, completing a BA in Religious Studies (UC Santa Barbara, 1996); an MA in Religious Studies (Graduate Theological Union, Berkeley, 1998); an MSt in the Study of Religion (University of Oxford, 2000); and a PhD in the Theology Faculty of the University of Oxford (2004). His published PhD thesis is on image worship in the Chaitanya Vaishnava tradition of Hinduism:

Attending Krsna's Image: Caitanya Vaisnava Murti-Seva as Devotional Truth (London and New York: Routledge, 2005). Based in Oxford, he is a Research Fellow of the Oxford Centre for Hindu Studies and is a regular Visiting Scholar at the Chinese University of Hong Kong. He continues to act in a ministerial capacity under the auspices of ISKCON.

Index

Other titles published by Arktos:

Beyond Human Rights
by Alain de Benoist

Manifesto for a European Renaissance
by Alain de Benoist & Charles Champetier

The Problem of Democracy
by Alain de Benoist

Revolution from Above
by Kerry Bolton

The Fourth Political Theory
by Alexander Dugin

Fascism Viewed from the Right
by Julius Evola

Notes on the Third Reich
by Julius Evola

Metaphysics of War
by Julius Evola

The Path of Cinnabar
by Julius Evola

Archeofuturism
by Guillaume Faye

Convergence of Catastrophes
by Guillaume Faye

Why We Fight
by Guillaume Faye

The WASP Question
by Andrew Fraser

War and Democracy
by Paul Gottfried

The Saga of the Aryan Race
by Porus Homi Havewala

Homo Maximus
by Lars Holger Holm

The Owls of Afrasiab
by Lars Holger Holm

De Naturae Natura
by Alexander Jacob

The Biocentric Worldview
by Ludwig Klages

Fighting for the Essence
by Pierre Krebs

Can Life Prevail?
by Pentti Linkola

Germany's Third Empire
by Arthur Moeller van den Bruck

Guillaume Faye and the Battle of Europe
by Michael O'Meara

The Ten Commandments of Propaganda
by Brian Anse Patrick

A Handbook of Traditional Living
by Raido

The Agni and the Ecstasy
by Steven J. Rosen

The Jedi in the Lotus
by Steven J. Rosen

It Cannot Be Stormed
by Ernst von Salomon

Tradition & Revolution
by Troy Southgate

Against Democracy and Equality
by Tomislav Sunic

The Arctic Home in the Vedas
by Bal Gangadhar Tilak

The Initiate: Journal of Traditional Studies
by David J. Wingfield (ed.)

Lightning Source UK Ltd.
Milton Keynes UK
UKOW04f1921070116

266023UK00006B/357/P